The Re-Emerging Securities Market in China

The Re-Emerging Securities Market in China

MEI XIA, JIAN HAI LIN,
AND
PHILLIP D. GRUB

QUORUM BOOKS
Westport, Connecticut • London

Library of Congress Cataloging-in-Publication Data

Xia, Mei.
  The re-emerging securities market in China / Mei Xia, Jian Hai
Lin, and Phillip D. Grub.
   p. cm.
  Includes bibliographical references and index.
  ISBN 0–89930–755–8 (alk. paper)
   1. Securities—China. 2. Finance—China. I. Lin, Jian Hai.
II. Grub, Phillip Donald. III. Title.
HG5788.X53 1992
332.63′2′0951—dc20   92–9824

British Library Cataloguing in Publication Data is available.

Library of Congress Catalog Card Number: 92–9824
ISBN: 0–89930–755–8

First published in 1992

Quorum Books, 88 Post Road West, Westport, CT 06881
An imprint of Greenwood Publishing Group, Inc.

Printed in the United States of America

The paper used in this book complies with the
Permanent Paper Standard issued by the National
Information Standards Organization (Z39.48–1984).

10 9 8 7 6 5 4 3 2 1

This book is dedicated to our parents, who made many sacrifices so that we might obtain an education and thereby contribute to the betterment of humanity and an enhanced understanding of people throughout the world. Their encouragement was a driving spirit that has had a tremendous impact on our lives.

Contents

Tables and Figures   ix

Preface   xi

1. Introduction   1

2. Economic Reforms and Their Impact on the Emergence of the Securities Market   19

3. Financial Sector Developments   35

4. The Emergence of the Securities Market   57

5. Securities Market Participants   69

6. Bond Issuing Activities   81

7. Stock Issuing Activities   93

8. Securities Trading Activities and Exchanges   103

9. Prospects for Future Development   117

Appendix I: Equity Markets in Economic Development   131

Appendix II: A Survey on Bond and Stock Issuances in China   149

Appendix III: Interim Regulations on the
               Administration of Bonds of Enterprises   167

Bibliography   173

Index   181

Tables and Figures

TABLES

1.1	A Profile of Emerging Securities Markets	2
1.2	Distribution of Financial Savings, 1985	10
3.1	Major Functions of Financial Institutions in China	44
3.2	Interbank Market Activities Reports	51
4.1	Total Outstanding of Financial Instruments, 1981–90	62
5.1	Gross Value of Industrial Output by Enterprises, 1978–88	70

FIGURES

1.1	Composition of the Emerging Markets	7
1.2	Market Capitalization in Selected Countries	8
1.3	Cumulative Returns of Emerging Securities Markets	8
1.4	Shares of World GDP, 1989	13
1.5	Shares of Market Capitalization, 1990	13
2.1	Financing of Domestic Investment, 1981–88	30
3.1	Individual Deposit Rates	40
3.2	Institutional Deposit Rates	40

3.3	Treasury Bond Rates	41
3.4	Interest Rates of Financial and Construction Bonds	41
4.1	Issues of Government Bonds by Holders, 1981–90	63
4.2	Issues of Other Government Bonds by Holders, 1981–90	64
5.1	Line of Business of Securities Issuers	75
5.2	Forms of Ownership of Securities Issuers	76
5.3	Number of Years in Operation	77
5.4	Financial Performance of Securities Issuers	78
5.5	Sources of Funds of Securities Issuers	78
6.1	Funds Raised Through Bonds	84
6.2	Maturities of Bonds	85
6.3	Interest Rates of Bonds	86
6.4	Types of Bond Buyers	89
6.5	Uses of Funds Raised Through Bond Issues	90
7.1	Purposes of Issuing Stocks	96
7.2	Types of Stock Buyers	97
7.3	Determination of Dividend Payments	98
7.4	Returns on Stocks	98

Preface

Being an agent of change is always a difficult task. The situation is even more complicated as one attempts to create change in a socialist economy such as China's, where there are no examples or role models to follow. Consequently, the Chinese leadership has embarked, since 1979, on an untrodden course whereby it has sought to enact reforms that would introduce elements of a market-driven economy into a socialist political environment. However, adaptations of economic policies cannot take place without altering certain existing political processes. As a consequence, with no precedent and where traditional economic and monetary theories have placed limited importance on the financial sector in comparison to other factors in the process of furthering economic development, the challenge of transforming China's massive economy into a dynamic entity that will be internally consistent as well as externally competitive is enormous, particularly if this is to be accomplished in the short term in order to meet head-on the forces of global competitiveness in the twenty-first century.

Prior to the open-door policy of 1979, China was primarily a barter economy in terms of its external relations with other countries. Furthermore, the number of trading partners was limited and there were virtually no foreign investment inflows. Since 1979, however, that has all changed. Foreign investment inflows, with the exception of a slight downturn in 1989 following the Tiananmen Square incident, continue to be major sources of new capital, technology, and management that are altering the face of the business sector. In 1991, foreign direct investment in China exceeded U.S. $10 billion, an increase of 50 percent over 1990, with the majority of the investment coming from Japan and the United States. However, to continue to attract foreign direct investment, it is essential that massive infrastructural developments take place to meet the needs of these foreign investors. Such developments depend upon high quality and efficient telecommunication systems, transportation networks, and adequate supplies of power. They also require streamlining existing bureaucracies so that decisions are made expeditiously, policies are consistent, legislation is clear concerning patents, copyrights and trademarks are enforced, and effective capital market systems are developed.

China is no longer in a position to finance all of its development needs solely through governmental action. Therefore, it will have to depend increasingly on equity financing from the private sector in the future if its goals for modernization are to be achieved. As a consequence, the need for an orderly, efficient, and competitive stock market is essential. Effective equity markets force corporations to compete on an equal basis for funds and open the horizon for entrepreneurs. Without an effective and operative securities market, companies must rely on internal financing through their retained earnings. In China, this is not possible even for the largest and most financially astute firms.

Furthermore, the existence of an equity market can serve to make the financial system more competitive and efficient. China's household savings rate is one of the world's highest, about 40 percent of disposable income, generating a pool of private savings valued at 1 trillion yuan. Securities compete with bank deposits, which may be subject to interest rate controls. In turn, this exerts pressure to keep the "controlled" interest rates closer to the more realistic "market" rates, which tend to reflect both inflation and scarcity of funds. Furthermore, the absence of viable equity markets tends to increase the debt/equity ratios of corporations, thereby weakening their capital structure. This endangers not only

their long-term viability, but also the solvency of their lenders in
the banking system as well as their international competitiveness.
In addition, the development of a viable equity market will tend to
force the banking community to be more efficient and competitive
both in terms of attracting deposits and in making loans, thereby
enhancing the financial posture of the nation's financial institutions.

Despite all the benefits derived from a healthy equity market,
the development of such a market also involves risks and costs if
it is not properly developed and regulated. Certain problems
inherent within the economic system of a nation cannot be avoided,
such as the inevitability of market cycles as well as a loss of control
over the financial system. Furthermore, the possibility of speculation and dishonest activities is always present. As a consequence,
the need for sound regulation is as paramount as the need for sound
legislation in establishing the equity markets.

In this book, the authors have sought to lay the groundwork for
the establishment of an orderly, efficient equity market that will
foster China's overall economic development and growth. The
transition from the pre-1979 "closed-door" policy to the emergence of an "open-door" policy from 1979 through mid-1991 has
been outlined. Included is an analysis of the economic reforms and
their impact on the emergence of the securities market, financial
sector developments, securities market participants, bond and
stock issuing activities, and securities trading activities as they
emerge and exist at present. Furthermore, an indepth look is taken
at the Shanghai securities exchange, the most formally developed
exchange in China, as well as the prospects for future development.

Since this book was written, many changes have taken place in
China. The trading activities on the stock markets in Shanghai and
Shenzhen have increased, and for the first time, foreign investors
have been allowed to participate in these markets. While these
markets remain thin, with eight companies listed on the Shanghai
exchange and six on the Shenzhen, plans to double the shares
floated on both markets have been announced. Additionally, a new
market may open in Guangzhou by the end of 1992. However, the

issues confronting investors in China and Chinese officials that are discussed in this book remain the same. Concerns about the regulation and stability of China's stock markets continue to be foremost in the minds of investors as they watch China develop its financial markets.

The text also contains a survey on bond and stock issuances as well as the interim regulations on the administration of bonds and enterprises in China. As such, this book is not only a pioneering effort exploring the emerging securities market in China, but also provides a reference base for future development of the equity markets and offers suggestions for China's leadership in furthering positive change that will in turn enhance the nation's growth, make the economy more attractive for foreign investors, and enhance overall prosperity for the Chinese people.

The authors are indebted to the numerous Chinese officials who gave up their valuable time to assist us in our endeavors. Interviews included senior bank and security exchange personnel, leading economists, corporate executives, and academicians. In addition, many senior officials of both the central and local governments contributed their views in off-the-record sessions. We are also indebted to the numerous individuals who completed the survey questionnaires that were essential to the study. Without the cooperation of these and other individuals, this book could not have been written.

We would also like to take this opportunity to thank Catherina Z. Tonson for her assistance in preparing the manuscript, as well as Damaris W. King, Aryamehr research assistant, and Yu Bowei. Their efficiency, diligence, and eye for detail contributed significantly.

1

Introduction

OVERVIEW

There are at least 30 emerging securities markets scattered throughout developing countries in Asia, Latin America, the Middle East, and Africa, each with marked differences in their levels of development. The origins of some markets date back to the nineteenth century and the beginning of industrialization; other markets originated in colonies where most of the trading took place within the large expatriate communities. The majority of emerging markets, however, were established between the two world wars and, in particular, during the postwar period as noted in Table 1.1.

The degree to which developing countries utilize securities markets to raise funds for long-term investment is determined by domestic economic and social conditions. Almost all high- and middle-income developing countries, as classified by the World Bank, have had securities markets, whereas only five countries in the low-income category have established securities markets.[1] Consequently, higher per capita incomes are essential in order to generate the necessary levels of savings available for discretionary investment.

The economic policies of each government, combined with the strategies set to implement them, are equally important factors in security market development. As illustrated in many studies (Ap-

Table 1.1
A Profile of Emerging Securities Markets

Country	GNP per capita (in U.S. dollar) (1988)	The year or period of market establishment
Low-income Economies		
Nigeria	290	
India	340	1877
Kenya	370	1954
Pakistan	350	1948
Sri Lanka	420	--
Middle-income Economies		
Morocco	830	1929-1967
Philippines	630	1927
Egypt	660	1883-1975
Cote d'Ivoire	770	1974
Zimbabwe	650	1896-1975
Thailand	1000	1975
Peru	1300	1860-1950
Turkey	1280	1850-1929
Ecuador	1120	1969
Tunisia	1230	--
Costa Rica	1690	1976
Columbia	1180	1928-1980
Chile	1510	1892-1973
Jordan	1500	1978
Brazil	2160	1900-1960
Uruguay	2470	1860-?
Portugal	3650	--
Malaysia	1940	1937-1973
South Africa	2290	--
Mexico	1760	1894-1976
Argentina	2520	1854-1982
Korea	3600	1920-1956
Venezuela	3250	1947
Greece	4800	--
Israel	8050	--
Trinidad & Tobago	3350	1966-1981
Hong Kong	9220	1891-1969
Singapore	9070	1930-1973
Taiwan	--	1962
High-income Exporters		
Kuwait	13400	1952-1973

Sources: World Bank, <u>World Development Report 1990</u>. New York: Oxford University Press, 1990; and Antoine W. van Agtmael, <u>Emerging Securities Market</u>, London: EUROMONEY Publications, 1984.

Note: "--" indicates non-availability of the data.

pendix I), these factors have been shown to have a pervasive impact on the activities and dynamics of various securities markets. For example, if investment allocation through financial markets was not considered important, if distortions and inefficiencies were overlooked, and if domestic savings mobilization was not a top priority, then securities markets would not have the opportunity to emerge, develop, and mature.

The availability and infusion of external capital is an important element in creating a viable securities market. In the early stages of a country's economic development, the demand for investment funds is often consistently high and generally well above the supply of domestic savings. This commonly results in a substantial resource gap, which must be financed through foreign borrowing. From the early 1960s to mid-1980s, for example, while a large portion of investment in developing countries was financed by domestic savings, a good share was financed by external capital. It should be noted that in industrial countries, savings actually exceeded domestic investment requirements by about three percentage points during the same period,[2] thereby freeing capital to be invested elsewhere.

In the early 1950s, the United States took the lead in initiating formal programs of foreign aid for developing countries. Later, other industrial countries followed with similar programs. The World Bank also shifted its focus from the reconstruction of Europe to the development of less developed countries. The International Finance Corporation (IFC) was established in 1956 to provide loans and equity investment to assist the development of the private sector in developing countries.

In the early 1960s, the International Development Association (IDA) was formed to provide a multilateral source of long term concessional financing for low-income countries. This period also saw the establishment of several regional development banks, including the African Development Bank, the Inter-American Development Bank, and the Asian Development Bank. Their major functions were to raise long-term financing and to mobilize financial resources to assist in the economic development of member countries in their respective regions.

During the period from 1973 to 1982, the amount of external financing flowing into developing countries increased dramatically. The most striking feature of this growth was the surge in lending by commercial banks through the Eurocredit market.[3] As a result, both the gross and net debt of developing countries increased sharply. With the slowdown in the world economy and high level of interest rates in the early 1980s, the over-reliance on external debt financing by developing countries became painfully evident. Many developing countries experienced debt-servicing difficulties caused by poor domestic economic policies and the deterioration of the external economic environment. The link between foreign borrowing and growth became more complex than had been expected. Moreover, many indebted countries realized that, due to their weakened repayment abilities, it was unlikely that they would be able to secure an additional supply of external funds from private foreign sources.

Since the international debt crisis in the early 1980s, many countries have realized that the impact of foreign borrowing has two possible outcomes: to promote economic growth and help an economy adjust to internal and external shocks; or to fund inefficient investments and permit a government to delay essential economic adjustments. In the latter case, the accumulation of external debt can make an economy more vulnerable to financial pressures from the world economy. More importantly, many countries have realized that the correct role of external financing is to supplement domestic savings, not to serve as a substitute for domestic savings. They have come to understand that in spite of the availability of external capital, efforts to raise domestic savings would have to remain essential if economic development were to be sustained.

Recent history has led to a growing disillusionment with the resource allocations of central government planners, the inefficiency of government-owned and -controlled enterprises, and the stranglehold that commercial banks often have over both the economy and the financial system of many developing countries. There has been an increasing awareness of the need to encourage the development and dynamism of the private sector. Many developing countries have gradually realized the urgent need to expand and deepen their domestic capital markets, to raise the rate of domestic private savings, and to allocate those savings more efficiently through the development and effective use of capital markets. In spite of the various obstacles inherent in their low level of economic development and in the weak institutional structure and infrastructure of their financial industry, many developing countries have found that the establishment of well-regulated securities markets results in a positive contribution to the economic development.

In more recent years, even formerly centrally planned economies, such as China and Hungary, whose development policies have traditionally emphasized government intervention and planned allocation of financial resources, have begun experimenting with the development of domestic securities markets. China, in particular, has achieved notable progress in this respect.

During the past decade, international finance has been revolutionized in most of the world as former standards of financial prudence for government and business have given way to new concepts with the focus shifting from loans to securities and from debt to equity.[4] The frontiers of international investment are beginning to push toward the major emerging markets of developing countries. This has, in part, been the result of a rapid growth of pension funds and mutual funds in the United States, Europe, and Japan, as well as in some of the newly industrializing countries. International money managers increasingly recognize the potential for risk diversification, higher returns, and other special benefits of moving into undiscovered markets and securities.[5] For developing countries, there is a growing sense of economic interdependence, combined with the urgency of stepping out from under the debt crisis and a growing recognition of the potential contribution that non-bank sharing can make to the growth of investment. In turn, this is causing a change in attitude of the more astute leaders

in countries that were previously closed or were difficult to pene-
trate by foreign investors.

On the other hand, as developing countries grow and as the
structures of their economies change, their relationships within the
global economy increasingly resemble those of the industrial
countries. As industry expands, exports shift from primary to
manufactured products, and as the domestic financial system
matures, many developing countries have increased their ability to
exploit opportunities in international financial markets, particularly new and diversified sources of financing, foreign portfolio
investment, and direct participation in the Euro-equity market. In
recent years, the share of equity and bond markets in international
finance has increased rapidly while the importance of traditional
bank credits declined. This trend is likely to accelerate as heavily
indebted countries recover from the debt crisis of the 1980s and
their market conditions improve.

Regional Composition of the Emerging Markets

Emerging securities markets are concentrated primarily in Asia
(72 percent as of the end of 1990; see Figure 1.1), particularly in
East Asian countries (46 percent). This reflects the region's rapid
economic development of the past two decades and its fast-devel-
oping financial markets. Although many Latin American countries
have suffered external debt problems during the past decade, their
domestic securities markets have remained large in size. The markets
in the Middle East and Africa captured only 2 percent of the total
emerging market share, reflecting the relatively low economic development level and unstable market conditions in these countries.

Market Size

No emerging securities market can compare in size with the
developed equity markets of Japan and the United States in terms
of market capitalization. However, the emerging markets are not
as small as is generally believed. Figure 1.2 provides market

Figure 1.1
Composition of the Emerging Markets (market capitalization, in percent, end 1990)

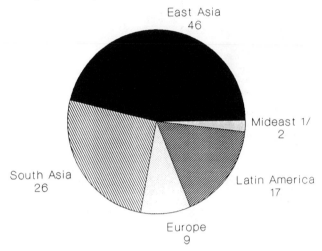

East Asia
46

Mideast 1/
2

Latin America
17

Europe
9

South Asia
26

Source: IFC, Emerging Stock Markets Factbook, 1991
1/ Including Africa.

capitalization for some of the world's developed equity markets and emerging markets, demonstrating that some large emerging equity markets such as those of Taiwan, Korea, Malaysia, and Brazil are comparable in size to a significant number of developed equity markets. Still, many emerging securities markets have demonstrated a more rapid growth rate than most of the developed markets during the 1980s.

Quality and Visibility

Many emerging markets have had a history of remarkable returns. Figure 1.3 presents a series of total return indexes expressed in U.S.

Figure 1.2
Market Capitalization in Selected Countries (in millions of dollars, end 1990)

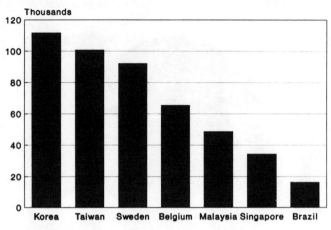

Source: Same as Figure 1.1.

Figure 1.3
Cumulative Returns of Emerging Securities Markets (in US$, December 1984 = 100)

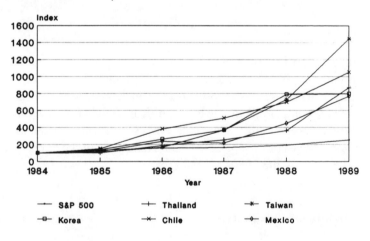

Source: Same as Figure 1.1.

dollars for a group of emerging markets. This series of indexes shows the high rates of return that could have been achieved by investors in some of these markets. Indeed, many of these markets, notably in Taiwan, Chile, Mexico, and Korea, outperformed the S&P 500 by a large margin between 1984 and 1989.

In addition to seeking high returns for individual assets, international institutional investors are also concerned with diversification. Diversification of assets among different countries and industries can either increase returns for a given level of risk, or reduce the risk for a given level of return. In many emerging markets correlation coefficients with the United States and other industrialized markets have proven to be extremely low, and in most cases close to zero. This provides excellent diversification opportunities for international investors. The potential investment opportunities provided by the emerging markets as well as the associated difficulties in actually utilizing them are beginning to draw worldwide attention.

Market Information and Investor Protection

Traditionally, emerging markets have been thought of as very small, lacking in liquidity and without significant disclosure, information, and investor protection. Some of these problems still exist in many emerging markets, but on a much smaller scale than generally expected. In fact, some markets, particularly in Korea, Malaysia, and Thailand, are of fairly high quality. Many countries provide specific country funds through which investments can be made by foreigners without being exposed to major risks.

Financial System and the Equity Market

Table 1.2 presents a general view of the financial market structure in selected developing countries, indicating the relative sizes of their financial sectors, including financial institutions, markets, and other instruments. It is evident that within the overall financial sector, with the exception of Malaysia and Chile, institutional

Table 1.2
Distribution of Financial Savings, 1985
(All figures represent percentages of total gross liabilities of the financial system)

	Central banks	Commercial banks	Savings banks and thrifts	Specialized lending institutions	Provident & pension funds	Insurance companies	Mutual funds trusts and investment banks	Total system assets (as % GNP)	Memo Items: Long-term debt securities & equities[1] (& system assets)	Equities (% system assets)
Developed markets										
U.S.	3	30	17	12	19	13	6	207	66	28
Canada	2	35	12	3	25	13	11	208	43	24
Sweden	6	31	10	27	13	12	1	231	54	15
Japan	3	36	29	13	1	8	10	300	43	20
Germany	6	21	37	20	0	13	3	224	42	13
Australia	7	27	20	21	11	14	1	158	50	27
France	7	53	13	12	1	7	6	218	19	6
United Kingdom	2	37	16	1	20	20	5	211	51	32
Singapore[2]	12	42	6	6	16	2	17	399	32	14
Emerging markets										
Venezuela	22	43	8	27	0	1	0	125	9	2
Taiwan	21	51	24	0	0	2	3	202	11	9
Korea	10	54	5	16	0	4	11	230	11	4
Argentina	35	47	1	12	0	5	0	125	11	4
Malaysia	10	45	5	18	16	3	4	232	48	24

Brazil	35	31	10	15	2	1	5	210	30	17
Argentina	35	47	1	12	0	5	0	125	11	4
Malaysia	10	45	5	18	16	3	4	232	48	24
Brazil	35	31	10	15	2	1	5	210	30	17
Jordan	19	59	0	21	0	1	0	221	30	24
Chile	20	63	0	2	11	5	1	115	40	14
Thailand	19	59	7	15	0	1	0	121	20	4
Nigeria	28	57	0	2	1	3	9	83	24	5
Philippines	35	40	4	16	0	3	3	120	16	3
India	13	55	7	8	7	9	1	74	31	12

Sources: Annual reports and periodic bulletins of central banks, national credit councils, central statistical offices, supervisory agencies, industry associations; and IFC staff estimates.

Note: The often unique roles some financial institutions play and differences in national statistical reporting have required some judgement on allocating liabilities. The percentages shown here should therefore be viewed only as indicators of approximate degrees of relative size.

[1] Long-term debt securities include goverment, agency and corporate securities with original maturities of one year or more, valued at par. Equities represent the market value of listed shares.

[2] Mutual funds and investment banks includes local and foreign merchant and investment banks' regional activities in Singapore.

investors are often relatively small in these countries. Major institutional investors in developing countries—pension funds, insurance companies, and mutual funds—typically play only a minor role in developing the securities markets, whereas in developed countries they normally play a critical role in forming the secondary markets for securities. This phenomenon partially explains why the 20 leading developing countries that represent about 10 percent of world GDP (Gross Domestic Product) account for only 5 percent of the total capitalization of the world equity market (Figures 1.4–1.5). This also suggests that most emerging markets have a substantial potential role for further growth.

It is recognized that there are indeed investment restrictions on foreign portfolio investment in most developing countries. However, the trend is clearly toward gradual liberalization and internationalization of these markets. The markets in Taiwan, Korea, Malaysia, Chile, and Thailand are already relatively open, while others have become accessible through a variety of country funds as mentioned earlier. In terms of the taxes on the returns of these investments, the withholding taxes in most of these countries are likely to be brought in line with the international average very soon. Although further liberalization and improvement in market conditions are needed, investment restrictions no longer present a serious barrier to many emerging markets.

Individual Case Studies on Emerging Markets

Antoine W. van Agtmael, formerly a group head and senior investment officer in the capital markets department of the IFC, conducted a comprehensive empirical study of the securities markets in 30 developing countries, which provided a good overview of the securities markets in these countries. The study contains a significant amount of information on the history of these markets, their sizes and activities, regulations, operations, and other technical aspects of these markets.[6]

In addition to his work, there have also been approximately a dozen studies on securities markets in individual countries, some

Figure 1.4
Shares of World GDP, 1989 (in percent)

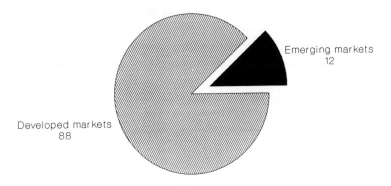

Emerging markets
12

Developed markets
88

Source: Same as Figure 1.1.

Figure 1.5
Shares of Market Capitalization, 1990 (in percent)

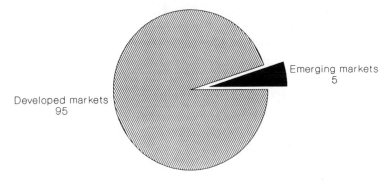

Emerging markets
5

Developed markets
95

Source: Same as Figure 1.1.

of which are listed in the Bibliography. These studies focus on various aspects of the emerging markets, from development process and operations and performance, to major policy issues. As demonstrated in these studies, the experience of developing countries with the development of securities markets varies widely from country to country. Most of these studies emphasize the importance of official recognition of the benefits of financial development through the development of securities markets and of the need to properly promote and regulate these markets.

Empirical works on securities markets in developing countries, however, seem to be inadequate, particularly those still at the initial development stage. There is also a lack of comparative studies on a number of issues, including (a) the relative significance of securities markets in countries at different stages of economic development; (b) the growth pattern of securities markets in different countries; and (c) the effectiveness of policies and measures to stimulate stronger financial deepening in countries at different development stages. An analytical framework with relatively reliable market indicators needs to be developed to facilitate comparative studies. Most importantly, none of the studies to date have dealt with the development of securities markets in centrally planned economies, either in Eastern Europe or in China.

Although the importance of securities markets has been recognized in a number of developing countries and increasing attention has been given to the development of these markets, they have generally not acquired a central role in the financial system. Until recently, securities markets in developing countries have been virtually unknown among the international financial community. They have been viewed by many as too small and too irrelevant to warrant much attention.

Purpose and Organization of the Book

Despite the much publicized political unrest in 1989, the past decade, on the whole, has seen dramatic changes in China's economy. Its economic structure has substantially changed and market forces have been allowed to function along with the central planning. The major objectives of the economic reform have been to reduce inefficiencies and distortions inherent in a purely centrally planned economy and to expedite economic development by improving allocative efficiency and relying on market forces and material incentives to motivate the desired economic behavior.

Along with economic reforms, China's financial system, which until recently was a monobank system, has undergone profound changes as well. The highly centralized system of investment policy decisions and single-channel vertical distribution of investment funds has been reformed, new financial institutions have been established, financial instruments have been created, and financial markets have been developed. However, the financial reform in China is still in its initial stage and changes in the financial system need to be better understood.

Purpose

This book is designed to provide a comprehensive analysis of China's new financial system and, in particular, the evolution and development of the securities market. The authors provide basic market information and analysis of China's emerging securities market with a view toward facilitating the understanding of the following issues: (a) Why did a securities market develop in China? (b) How do market practices compare with those in other countries? (c) What are the major difficulties and problems in the development process of the securities market? and (d) What growth potential may the Chinese securities market have?

The book is based primarily on field studies, supplemented by a questionnaire survey (Appendix II) and by many personal interviews with the Chinese officials and staff of the securities issuing companies and stock exchange centers. Specifically, three steps were taken during the research phase: (a) questionnaire designing; (b) field survey and personal interviews; and (c) literature review and research on information that could not be obtained through (a) and (b).

Since there were no systematic data available regarding the Chinese securities market, a questionnaire was designed to collect primary data and market information to facilitate the analyses in this book. To make the research more comprehensive, the questionnaire was divided into four parts. The first part was a general survey designed to obtain information on securities issuers, the size of their assets, operational history, financial position and performances, with a view toward providing a profile of the securities issuers in the Chinese market. The second part of the questionnaire was focused on bond issuing activities by participating companies. Twenty questions were prepared to obtain information concerning bond issuing activities, volume of issues, terms of issues (including interest rates and maturities), uses of funds, major buyers, experiences with these issuing activities, and restrictions encountered by issuers. The third part of the questionnaire concentrated on stock issuing activities. Questions similar to those in the bond section were presented to the issuing companies. The last part of the questionnaire was designed to examine the trading activities of bonds and stocks in the secondary markets in China, including operations, market characteristics, problems faced by secondary markets, and prospects.

The questionnaire was first prepared in English and then translated into Chinese and distributed to selected companies that had issued either bonds or stocks from 1985 through 1988. According to the data available, there were about 6,000 enterprises that had issued bonds or stocks at the time when the research was conducted. Issuing activities were initially concentrated in large cities such as Shenyang, Shanghai, and Guangzhou, and later spread out to various provinces and smaller cities. The survey, however, was focused primarily on the major cities, particularly Shanghai, where securities issuing activities were more active and the volume more significant than elsewhere in the country. The selection of enterprises was random, but to some extent selective, in the sense that efforts were made to include, wherever possible, issuers with different types of ownership status, businesses, and sizes. The sample base was selected to provide a comprehensive and inclusive picture of China's emerging securities market.

To augment the questionnaire survey, interviews were undertaken with managers of selected issuing enterprises, staff of trading centers, and officials in both central and local organizations who were in charge of the regulatory and administrative aspects of the securities market. These interviews, which are included in Chapter 9, provide a basis for understanding China's securities market and its operations as it re-emerges, with a view toward achieving China's modernization goals as the twenty-first century approaches.

NOTES

1. The World Bank defines low-income countries as those with a per capita GNP of $500 or less in 1988; middle-income countries as those with a per capita GNP of more than $500 but less than $6,000; and high-income countries as those with a per capita GNP of $6,000 or more in the same year. See World Bank, *World Development Report 1990* (New York: Oxford University Press, 1990).

2. World Bank, *World Development Report 1985* (New York: Oxford University Press, 1985), 12.

3. The Eurocredit market refers to a medium-term, floating-rate, and syndicated Euroloan market.

4. For a better understanding of the securitization of financial markets, see Tran Q. Hang, "The Securitization of International Finance," *Handbook of International Investment*, edited by Carl Beidleman (Probus Publishing Company 1987), 199–207; *International Capital Markets—Development and Prospects*, International Monetary Fund, April 1990; and *Determinants and Systemic Consequences of International Capital Flows*, Occasional Paper, International Monetary Fund, March 1991.

5. Brian L. Sudweeks, "Equity Market Development in Developing Countries: General Principles, Case Studies, Portfolio Implications and Relevance for the People's Republic of China," Ph.D. dissertation, George Washington University, 1987.

6. David Gill, "Global Investing—the Emerging Markets," paper presented at Council of Institutional Investors, Semi-annual Meeting in November 1987, 6.

2

Economic Reforms and Their Impact on the Emergence of the Securities Market

As most are aware, there is no precedent in the history of securities market development of a centrally planned economy fostering a securities market. This is true, to some extent, because public ownership and a non-market economy usually do not provide the conditions necessary for the development of a truly functional securities market.

Why then did a securities market emerge in China? Why has this market gradually gained momentum? These are important questions that need to be answered. Before responding to these questions, a brief review of the economic environment within which China's securities market has developed provides the background information essential to understanding this unique case. This chapter, therefore, is focused on the nature and extent of China's economic reforms since 1978 and their impact on the emergence of the securities market.[1]

ECONOMIC STRUCTURE BEFORE 1978

The previous economic system in China, during the pre-reform period (1949–1978), was formed during the years from 1953 through 1957 (first five-year plan), and was highly centralized. In the period immediately following the founding of the People's

Republic of China (1949), the level of the country's economic development was low and its existing economic structure was weak. Policy makers hoped that a centralized and planned economy, modeled after that of the Soviet Union, would enable them to assert direct control over aggregate demand and avoid possible economic crises after the war. To have an effective control over the economic activities and to practice the concepts of socialism, a tightly controlled economic system was designed with the following subsequent developments:

1. Private enterprises were first controlled, and then incorporated into state-owned enterprises;
2. Land was redistributed, then collectivized in 1955–56, and finally the commune system was established in rural areas in 1958;
3. The currency (Yuan) was made inconvertible and external trade was monopolized in order to insulate the economy from the possible external effect;
4. Investment was incorporated into the planning process with the state determining both the quantity and direction of investments;
5. The use of cash was restricted. Enterprises were forced to conduct most of their business through account transfers with state-owned banks; and
6. Private consumption was regulated by wage and price controls, commodity rationing schemes, and denial of consumer credit.

Under such a system, most production and investment decisions were made by the government. Government administrative agencies set production quotas for enterprises and provided supplies, including raw materials, production inputs, and, most of all, funds for capital investments to meet these quotas. Enterprises and their government sponsors were judged largely by the physical volumes of output produced. Profits were, in return, remitted to the state. Therefore, there was no sustaining linkage between an enterprise's efficiency and the benefits or losses accrued to those responsible for managing the enterprise. Supply and distribution channels were rigid and unresponsive to shifts in demand.

Although the economy recovered sharply and performed well during the early years, major problems began to emerge in the late 1950s and worsened throughout the following two decades. Economic growth was achieved largely through the application of greater amounts of physical inputs, capital, and manpower rather than more efficient use of resources. Prior to 1977, total productivity growth was zero or even slightly negative. Thus, the sacrifices required became disproportionate to the gains achieved. With the increased level of complexity in the economy, this system rapidly became too rigid and out of step with economic development. Its main defects were as follows:

1. There was no clear demarcation between the role of government and of enterprise. The government intervened excessively and directly in the management of enterprises that were administered by various central or local government agencies that formulated their plans for development without considering the actual requirements of the enterprises. The government dictated the production plans for the enterprises and controlled the transfer of raw material and other production inputs, the purchase of outputs, and the distribution of all labor. Such highly centralized administrative planning and heavy control failed to meet the needs of enterprises, thus causing enormous distortions and waste in resource allocation.

2. There was a disregard for the role of market forces, resulting in a dislocation between production and market, and an inability to alter plans to deal with changes in demand.

3. There was excessive egalitarianism in the distribution of income. Enterprises remitted most of their profits to the government, which also provided budgetary subsidies to cover all losses. Rewards for an enterprise and its workers had no bearing on their performance, resulting in enterprises "eating from the same big pot" of the state.

4. There were defects in the economic structure as well. The collective economy had not undergone proper development and the individual economy had been almost totally suppressed. Modes of operation were extremely uniform; that is, almost everything was operating under state ownership.

These defects seriously hampered the initiative and creativity of enterprises and workers alike and did serious harm to what would otherwise have been a vigorous economy. The consequences of overcentralization created a vicious circle: the more centralized the economy, the more rigid its structure; the less need for people to be creative; the more need for a centralized economy.

PROCESS OF ECONOMIC REFORMS

As a central element of its overall strategy to improve allocative efficiency and promote the sustained growth of the economy, the government decided in 1979 to carry out unprecedented experiments with economic reforms. The major goal of the reforms was to eliminate the enormous waste and inefficiency that had characterized the economy since the early 1950s. More specifically, the reforms were aimed at: (a) moving the economy toward greater decentralization of decision-making; (b) increasing reliance on market forces and on material incentives for motivating desired economic behavior and resource allocation; and (c) opening the economy to external competition through foreign investment.

The reforms were not carried out as a comprehensive program at one time. Rather, they were initiated and implemented as a series of experiments; sometimes nationwide, sometimes regional. Where specific reform measures were deemed effective, they were promoted and implemented comprehensively; while in other areas, the reforms were planned and carried out selectively. Although some aspects of the reform have remained controversial and the results have been mixed, undoubtedly the entire economy has gone through profound changes. In addition, the reforms have had significant impact on the financial sector, which led to the emergence and development of securities markets in later stages.

AGRICULTURAL REFORM

Reform measures were first introduced and have progressed the farthest in rural areas. The scope of agricultural reform touched almost all aspects of the agricultural sector, from its organization, production, pricing, and marketing to the allocation of labor between farm and non-farm sectors. The basic thrust of the reform was to decentralize production responsibility down to the household level. This was a departure from the core principle of collective farming under the commune system. Under the "household responsibility system," a family contracts a plot of land, and in return, it meets the state's procurement quota and pays to the state the agricultural tax and a fee for using the land. The family can retain any surplus products and sell the surplus in the free market at market-determined prices. Thus, the reward for individual efforts is linked closely to final output.

The government also adopted a series of important measures to promote agricultural production, including (a) increases in the purchase price of agricultural and sideline products and introduction of a premium price for products sold above the quota; (b) a significant reduction in the number of agricultural products for which the government had a monopoly in purchasing to give farmers a greater degree of autonomy in production; and (c) an exemption of agricultural tax for designated poor areas.[2]

The agricultural reform has been a tremendous success. The pace of agricultural growth since the reform has been unprecedented. Performances have been even more impressive in the non-grain crop sector. After two decades of sluggish growth, agricultural output has soared since 1978, before leveling off somewhat toward the end of the 1980s.

It is important to recognize that the remarkable growth since 1978 in the agricultural sector has been achieved without sharp increases in total farm inputs. Given increased employment opportunities in rural small-scale enterprises, the number of farmers engaged in farming has actually declined.[3] At the same time, the average per capita farm income in current prices increased sharply. There has been little doubt that the real income gains in rural areas during the past decade were substantial and have probably exceeded those achieved in the previous three decades combined.

INDUSTRIAL REFORM

In 1984 the focus of reform expanded to industrial sectors, the most challenging and difficult task of the overall reform efforts. The government document on "The Reforming of Economic Structure" issued in October 1984 signaled the beginning of a major push to alter significantly the system of Soviet-style economic central planning and to change the long-standing pattern of industrial planning and operations.

The specific objectives of the industrial reform were: (a) to increase industrial productivity by providing autonomy and incentives to enterprises; (b) to create markets for industrial inputs and outputs and to institute price reforms to correct distortions; (c) to strengthen commercial interactions between industrial enterprises and consumers and to make enterprise managers understand and behave in accordance with the rules of the market; and (d) to attract foreign capital, technology, and managerial expertise to further advance the country's economic development.

In essence, the goal of the industrial reform was to endow enterprises with "three Li's" or powers: Dongli (motivation), Yali (pressure), and Shili (strength). The reform was designed to provide enterprises with motivation to grow; expose them to both internal and external pressure (competition) of the marketplace to ensure efficient production; and give them strength or autonomy in terms of physical, financial, and human resources to sustain expansion and growth.

PLANNING AND PRICE REFORMS

Before 1978, highly centralized planning was mandatory and carried out in two parallel processes: the formulation of annual aggregate plans and individual project approvals. In this way, not only were the nation's overall economic development direction and priorities decided by the government planning agencies, but also the production quota for each enterprise was determined by the government administrators. The planning system itself had not generated an efficient pattern of investment; its shortcomings in this respect were a major factor motivating the economic reform.

In the course of the economic reform, the scope of mandatory planning was reduced while that of guidance planning was expanded. Planning was focused on outlining the general direction the national economy should take. At the same time, there was a substantial increase in the use of macroeconomic policy instruments such as taxation, credit, and interest rates. Only products essential to the national economy were kept under the state plan. Other products were more broadly regulated through guidance plans that provided the collective enterprises and private sector with more flexibilities and autonomies. More importantly, the private sector was allowed to re-emerge, grow, and compete with state- and collectively owned enterprises as well as among themselves. Although no statistics are available to gauge the importance of commodities under mandatory plans, it appears that they have comprised a much smaller share of the number of commodities as compared with those prior to the reform.

In the pre-reform period, prices had failed to play an allocative role in the economy due to the heavy reliance on administrative controls. Even until 1984, prices of most consumer goods and industrial raw materials, as well as the procurement prices of major agricultural commodities, were fixed by the state, and in many cases had changed little during the previous 30-year period. Prices were largely determined according to political and social considerations with no proper adjustment mechanism built in to reflect changes in income and demand. As such, the process of price determination neglected changes in productivity. Price determination also tended to produce a uniform consumer price for broadly similar products.

In late 1984 and early 1985, significant price reforms were initiated in the industrial sector. Since then, prices have been gradually reformed and are now basically established in one of three ways; (a) fixed prices set directly by the state and local governments; (b) "negotiated" prices between producers and users; and (c) "face prices" determined by market forces. Consequently, the proportion of transactions carried out at prices with some degree of flexibility has increased over time.

However, the price reform has by no means been complete. In fact, much of the price distortion from the pre-reform period remains and a close linkage between domestic and international prices has yet to be made. Following the surge in inflation during 1987–88, there was some re-entrenchment in the area of price reform as new focus was placed on bringing inflation under control. In 1988–89, it appeared that the government reverted to administrative measures to tighten price controls. As a result, state-fixed prices were more rigidly enforced and negotiated prices were more strictly observed. There were also indications that further price reforms were to be delayed.

DIVERSIFICATION OF THE ECONOMIC STRUCTURE

The widely recognized failure of the state enterprises to respond effectively to market conditions, to take sufficient advantage of the creativity of the work force, and to absorb the growing number of people looking for employment led the authorities to permit private business activities to take place. Indeed, an important element of economic reforms in both urban and rural areas was the proliferation and rapid growth of non-state forms of enterprise ownership and management. For example, between 1978 and 1988 the share of output of collectively owned enterprises rose from about 22 percent of the total to over 36 percent, while that of private enterprises (most of them are small in scale) grew virtually from zero to about 7 percent. In the service sector, the share of private and collective enterprises in output combined was even higher.

While the rise of non–state-owned enterprises that enjoyed more freedom than state enterprises during 1978–88 provided a source of competition and a significant impulse toward greater efficiency of the economy, these largely small-scale enterprises were hurt seriously by the "economic adjustment" program started in the latter part of 1988. Credit from state banks was substantially tightened and controls on operations were re-emphasized. As a result, many private-sector enterprises reportedly went bankrupt and their production was curtailed.

OPENING TO THE OUTSIDE WORLD

China had been isolated from the rest of the world for more than 30 years before it adopted an "open-door" policy in 1979. Due to both international and domestic historical reasons, China had a very limited scope of economic exchanges with the rest of the world and failed to take advantage of the available capital and technology in the Western countries.

Since 1979, significant steps have been taken to liberalize the external sector of the economy. These measures included: (a) decentralizing the trade system by giving local governments and enterprises more autonomy; (b) encouraging foreign direct investment inflows through relaxation of policies and controls; and (c) more actively utilizing external financing to supplement domestic savings.

The main thrust of the open-door policy called for vigorous expansion of foreign trade and absorption of foreign capital, advanced technology, and management. This policy was aimed at moving China from a closed economy based on small-scale agricultural production to a more open economy oriented toward industrial production. These reform measures resulted in a marked expansion of external trade, particularly exports; remarkable inflows of foreign investment; and a substantial increase in external borrowing.[4] Between 1978 and 1989, for example, exports increased by over threefold, while accumulated foreign investment amounted to about U.S. $20 billion. Although external debt rose sharply, total borrowing and debt service remained well below cautious levels (the debt service ratio in 1989, for example, was about 10 percent, far below the 20 percent cautious level).

Prior to 1979, the Chinese financial system resembled a monobank system in which all financial transactions were handled by a few specialized banks with a virtual absence of other financial institutions or financial markets. Under this system, all key financial resources were allocated according to central planning. The government budget was designed to supply all investment funds plus a minimum of working capital to enterprises. Fiscal appropriation charged no interest on the funds provided, nor did it require the repayment of the principals, since the state had full claim on all profits of enterprises. The role of the banking system was to provide the amount of credit to enterprises necessary to comply with government plans and to audit payments to ensure that funds were used for their designated purposes. Therefore, the banks' function in such a system was largely to accommodate the economy; or to put it more vividly, banks acted merely as the government's cashiers and played a limited intermediary role in the economy.[5]

The expansion of market functions in the economy after 1979 gave rise to the need for reform of the financial system. The Chinese government recognized that the requirements for an efficient financial system were not very different from those for an efficient system of production. Competition, responsibility for profits and losses, incentives for good performance, and rational pricing—in this case, interest rates—were basic elements of a more efficient financial system. The recognition of these requirements helped shape several important aspects of financial reform at a later stage. The goal of the financial reform, therefore, was to gradually establish a forceful and flexible banking system and a diversified financial sector that could help raise funds more effectively and use them more efficiently. More specifically, it was aimed at (a) changing the old investment system to improve the investment efficiency and returns on investment funds; (b) motivating the initiative of financial institutions in mobilizing and effectively using financial resources; (c) promoting the increase in savings from individual households; and (d) gradually correcting distortions in the financial market through interest rate adjustments based on market forces.[6]

Among all the measures taken, the first important step was to reduce the state budget's dominant role in resource allocation. Government investment expenditures, for example, declined from almost 40 percent of GNP in the late 1970s to about 23 percent in 1989. On the revenue side, the basis of government revenue was partly switched from profit remittances to income taxation. Non-tax revenue, which had been an important source of revenues reflecting profit remittance from state enterprises, has become negligible.

The second important change was that fiscal appropriations in most sectors of the economy were gradually replaced by interest-bearing loans. Only government departments, schools, and other non-profit units continued to be eligible for obtaining government budgetary funds as they could not generate funds to service loans by themselves.

The expansion of loans into areas once exclusively dominated by budgetary allocations was purposely designed to (a) make recipients of funds more responsible for the uses of the funds; and (b) make enterprise managers responsible for servicing debt through more careful financial planning and implementation of investment projects, so as to discourage them from requesting funds for projects with negative rates of return. Substituting grants with loans also meant that poorly managed enterprises now had to face tough loan terms or be denied any borrowing possibilities.

As a consequence of the above changes, the functions of the financial institutions were greatly strengthened and their business scope expanded. Along with the financial reform, the role of specialized banks and the nature of their operations were also altered in a number of ways: (a) they became increasingly important as a source of enterprise finance; (b) they gradually shifted their focus from being purely short-term lenders to providing more medium-term and fixed-asset financing; (c) they became lenders to non-state as well as state enterprises; and (d) they increasingly used interest rates as a tool of savings mobilization and resource allocation.

Recent statistics on the sources of investment capital in China reveal extensive changes in the financial relations of enterprises with the government. The state now provides less than 10 percent of all investment funds. Bank loans, which were not a major source of capital prior to 1979, account for about one-fifth of total investment requirement, while financing from other sources rose by about 65 percent (Figure 2.1).

HOW ENTERPRISES OPERATE IN THE NEW ENVIRONMENT

The purpose of the industrial reform was to change the economic environment within which enterprises operate so that they would become independent economic entities, responsible for their own profits and losses, and endowed to improve their efficiency and profitability. In this new environment, operations of enterprises were changed in several ways that are examined in detail below.

Managerial Accountability and Incentives

Prior to the reform, enterprises were required to turn over all of their profits to the state, and in return they obtained their

Figure 2.1
Financing of Domestic Investment, 1981–88 (percent of total)

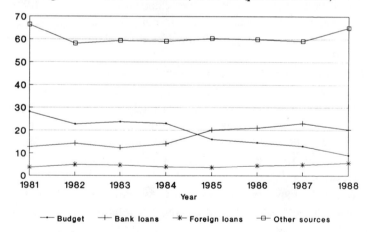

Source: China Statistical Yearbook, 1990

investment funds from the state. In that environment, there was no incentive for enterprises to grow or to alter their product structure in order to meet market demand. Rather, their primary objective was to fulfill the production target assigned by the government. For enterprises with good performance, the most they could earn from the government was an honorary recognition for their efforts.

After market elements were introduced in 1979, the government recognized that in order for enterprises to assume responsibility for their own performance, they must be given greater authority and incentives to work more efficiently. Most importantly, enterprise managers needed greater autonomy in production, procurement, marketing, and disposition of profit. In 1980 a profit retention system was introduced, and under this system enterprises were allowed to retain a certain portion of profits for both production and welfare purposes. Thus, enterprises were no longer required to remit all profits to the state. Later a corporate income tax system was introduced that required enterprises to pay income taxes instead of profit remittances. As a result of these changes, profits once again became the most important measure of an enterprise's performance, and enterprise managers became accountable for managing their enterprises.

Production and Marketing

In the past, state administrative agencies set production quotas for the enterprise and provided the supplies necessary to meet these quotas. The only direct contact between enterprises and customers occurred during annual national order meetings, where delivery schedules, type of goods available, and quality specifications were determined. Since customer orders were assigned by the state and products were distributed by wholesale agencies of the government, managers did not need to understand market needs and consumer preferences, or develop marketing and distribution skills.

While it is true that at present output targets are still set and many supplies are still provided by the government, the system has become more flexible. Enterprise managers, for example, can now source supplies independently to support above-quota productions, establish their own marketing channels, create brand reputation, and provide after-the-sale services. However, progress in product marketing and distribution has been slow, mainly due to the partial reform in the pricing system. As discussed earlier, while market forces are now allowed to play a role in determining prices, prices of a large amount of goods, particularly important raw materials and bulk commodities, are still administrated by the government. As such, still over half of industrial inputs and outputs are distributed at these administrated prices.

Personnel Management

The success or failure of the industrial reform will ultimately be determined on the shop floor where new managerial autonomy is exercised. Given the importance of the role of individuals in enterprise, significant changes have taken place in the system of professional job mobility and managerial appointments. In the past, enterprise managers were appointed by the technical or administrative bureaus overseeing the enterprise or, in the case of key enterprises, by the industrial ministries. Appointments were based on both technical and ideological credentials, but Party membership qualifications were the chief criterion used in determining professional positions. Today, some managers continue to be appointed by higher-level administrative agencies, but more managers are being appointed based on their technical qualifications and relevant experience within the enterprise.

Enterprise employees were traditionally assigned jobs by local labor bureaus, and neither the enterprise nor workers had much choice in these assignments. Today, labor bureaus still make most assignments, but enterprises with managerial autonomy can hire and fire workers under certain circumstances. Workers have also been granted greater mobility and school graduates have been encouraged to submit job applications to various employers. Managers have been given greater discretion to promote better and more qualified workers and to dismiss those who do not perform well.

Financial Control

Enterprise management in the pre-reform period involved practically no financial decisions being made by the enterprises' managers. Funds were allocated by the state to the enterprise and held in separate bank accounts for specified purposes. The remittance of profits to the government prevented any significant accumulation of cash reserves, and in any event, there were virtually no interest-bearing financial assets available for making use of temporary cash reserves.

Economic and financial reforms in the past decade have had a profound impact on the financial management of enterprises. Funds for enterprise investment now must be raised at interest from the financial system or from investors. Enterprises applying for investment funds must also be concerned about the financial viability of projects and are responsible for generating adequate cash flows to service debt. Approval of investment funds by the government at all levels is also increasingly based on project viability and the financial rate of return of the project.

As a consequence of the changes in the credit allocation system and the relative reduction in state investment funds, enterprises must seek other ways to finance their investment projects. When a significant amount of capital, in addition to that provided by the state, is needed for an investment project, enterprises now have several alternatives, including loans from banks, which are becoming an important source of needed funds. Equity and debt instrument issuances, while still uncommon, have emerged as another significant alternative. In other words, profit retention, greater managerial autonomy, and the growing availability and diversity of financial instruments have given greater importance to the financial management of enterprises, and have also given rise to the establishment of securities markets where enterprises can raise capital for investments.

NOTES

1. For example, see Huan Xiang, "Economic Reforms Finding Foothold in Town and Country," *Intertrade* (July 1985), 14. Also, a good review of economic reforms in China is found in "China, Economic Reforms and Macroeconomic Management," *IMF Occasional Paper No. 76*, 1991.

2. World Bank, *World Development Report 1986* (New York: Oxford University Press, 1986), 105.

3. William A. Fischer, "Update on Enterprise Reforms," *The China Business Review* (Sept.–Oct. 1986), 42–45.

4. See Phillip Donald Grub and Jian Hai Lin, *Foreign Direct Investment in China* (Westport, Conn.: Quorum Books, 1991), 77–82.

5. Bian Fa, "Reform—China's Second Revolution," *China Reconstructs* (October 1987), 18.

6. For a good review of the financial sector reform, see Cecil R. Dipchang, Colin Dodds, Patricia McGraw, and Keng Chen, "Emerging Trends in China's Financial Sector," *Asia Pacific Journal of Management*, Vol. 8, No. 1 (1991), 35–54.

3

Financial Sector Developments

Recent changes and developments in China's financial sector have been significant. Given the many changes that have taken place in China's financial sector in the past decade, a better understanding of the new financial environment can be achieved by focusing on the following issues: (a) major tasks of China's financial reform; (b) new changes in key areas of the financial sector; (c) recent developments in the financial market; and (d) constraints on the overall development of the financial sector.

MAJOR TASKS OF CHINA'S FINANCIAL REFORM

Replacing Direct Administrative Control with Indirect Economic Means

In the pre-reform period, the traditional tools for implementing monetary policy available to market economies such as open market operations, manipulation of reserve requirements, and changing discount rates were not available in China. Monetary policy was implemented by explicit financial planning. The major objective of financial planning, which was composed of the government budget, the credit plan and the cash plan, was to supply the quantity of money and credit required to satisfy transactional needs arising from efforts to fulfill state economic development plans.[1]

With the introduction of market functions into the economic system in 1979, there was an increasing need to replace direct administrative control with indirect economic means for macro-economic management. This would necessitate increased dependence on the manipulation of interest rates, reserve requirements, open-market operations, and other monetary policies to attain macroeconomic objectives. The government's decision to move toward the use of indirect means of monetary controls was consistent with the efficiency objectives of the economic reform, as it has been proven that centrally planned economies that use direct controls to achieve monetary and credit targets have suffered from undesirable effects of such policies.[2]

Reforming the Management of Existing Financial Institutions and Diversifying the Financial System

The Chinese financial system was highly centralized prior to 1978, with financial institutions consisting of a few large state-owned banks that were tightly controlled by the central government to carry out economic plans and perform specific financial functions. The principal institution was the People's Bank of China (PBC), which functioned as both the central bank and a commercial bank. Other financial institutions included the Agricultural Bank of China (ABC), the Construction Bank of China (CBC), the Bank of China (BOC), and the People's Insurance Company (PIC).[3] Each functioned specifically in its area of responsibility. State enterprises were required to hold their money in the form of deposits in these banks, which monitored and cleared all inter-enterprise transactions. The PBC also offered savings deposits for households. A major task of the financial reform was to make banks play the role they should have played in mobilizing savings and allocating financial resources efficiently, rather than playing the role of government bookkeepers and cashiers. In addition, the diversification of the financial system, by promoting the establishment of other non-bank financial institutions such as contractual savings, has been widely recognized as crucial to the increased efficiency and competitiveness of China's financial system.

Developing Financial Markets

Financial markets have developed in most modern economies to permit the buying and selling of financial instruments, including equity shares. A well-developed financial market offers savers and borrowers a wide range of asset and liability options, enabling them to meet their respective objectives. At the same time these options make macroeconomic control through market mechanisms by the central bank an easier job. The development of China's financial sector depends heavily on the development of financial markets, including short-term money markets and long-term capital markets, which will facilitate the free flow of funds and help correct price distortions in the credit market.

Modernizing Financial Facilities and Infrastructure

There is a tremendous need to modernize China's financial infrastructure and facilities in order to offer its citizens the basic banking and financial services available in any modern economy such as check writing, debit cards, credit cards, and 24-hour ATM service. There is also a desperate need for China to develop its computerized information systems in order for financial institutions to provide more and better services, to provide timely information, and to automate some of the banking operations.

These remain the major tasks China must undertake to improve the functions of its financial system so that it can contribute to national economic development by effectively and efficiently mobilizing savings and allocating resources in keeping with the modernization goals set forth in 1979.

NEW CHANGES IN CHINA'S FINANCIAL SECTOR

The Establishment of the Central Banking System

The decentralization of decision making to state-owned enterprises and financial institutions necessitates the development of indirect controls on monetary aggregates. In 1984 the People's Bank of China was designated as the country's central bank responsible for designing and implementing monetary policies. The commercial banking activities of the PBC were consequently assigned to newly created specialized banking institutions. Since its transformation into the central bank, the PBC has had at its disposal four major monetary policy instruments: (1) credit to the specialized banks; (2) ceilings on the credit extended by the specialized banks; (3) reserve requirements for the specialized banks; and (4) control over the structure of interest rates.[4]

The PBC's credit to the specialized banks has become the most prominent instrument of monetary policy. There are two types of such credit: (a) credit extended by the PBC head office to each specialized bank's head office, consistent with projected developments in the bank's lending and deposit operations (the specialized banks' head offices have discretion over the allocation of this credit to their various branches located in the provinces and large cities); and (b) temporary PBC credit, which has become a significant source of funds for branches of specialized banks since 1985, and is extended by provincial branches and city-level sub-branches of the PBC to the corresponding levels of the specialized banks, subject to a limit set by the PBC head office on the total amount of temporary credit allocated to each province to cope with the fluctuations in demand and supply conditions.

In the pre-reform period, when the PBC extended credit directly to enterprises, ceilings on the extension of credit to various economic sectors under a comprehensive credit plan had constituted the principal instrument of monetary policy. Since 1985, ceilings on the total credit of each specialized bank have been implemented as a principal means of credit control. In addition, subceilings have been specified for the ceilings on the credit extended by the specialized banks and for fixed investment loans and credit to rural enterprises.

Currently, the specialized banks are required to redeposit a specified portion of their deposit liabilities with the PBC. During 1984, the redeposit rates (or reserve requirement ratio) were set at 40 percent of urban household deposits, 20 percent of enterprise deposits, and 25 percent of rural deposits. Since January 1985, these redeposit ratios have been reduced to an uninformed 10 percent.[5]

More recently, the central bank has also used refinancing rates as an important instrument to influence monetary aggregates. Using this approach, the central bank mainly finances the specialized banks primarily by providing credit loans. In this situation, the refinancing rate is similar to the rediscount rate in terms of macroeconomic regulation and controls. At the same time, increased use has been made of interest rates at the commercial banking level to promote efficient utilization of funds and mobilization of savings. Since 1982, interest rates have been progressively raised, from the very low levels that prevailed since the 1950s, to reflect more closely the supply of and demand for credit (see Figures 3.1–3.4). Equally important, interest rates that apply to individual and institutional borrowers have gradually become unified.

However, there still exists a variety of preferential rates for business activities that are designated as a high priority or where profitability is low because of the prevailing distorted price structure. Floating rates for certain loans (including ABC loans, PBC credit for technical innovation, and BOC foreign trade credit) were introduced in late 1984. Subject to PBC approval, the specialized banks can currently adjust these rates by up to one-fifth above or below the administered rates set by the PBC.

However, the achievement of an independent central bank in China has proved to be difficult during this period of economic transition. Although the monetary control instruments are now

Figure 3.1
Individual Deposit Rates (in percent)

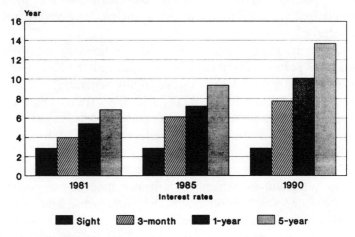

Source: Information gathered from
various sources.

Figure 3.2
Institutional Deposit Rates (in percent)

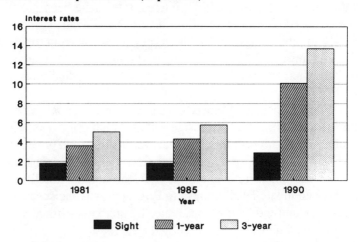

Source: Information gathered from
various sources.

40

Figure 3.3
Treasury Bond Rates (in percent)

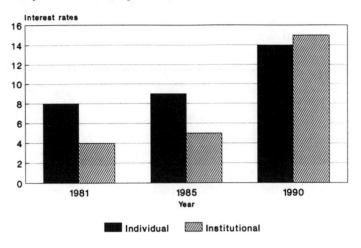

Source: Information gathered from
various sources.

Figure 3.4
Interest Rates of Financial and Construction Bonds (in percent)

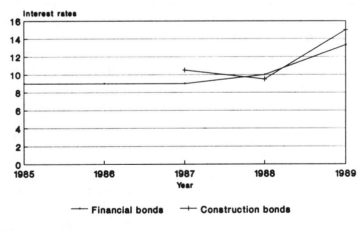

Source: Information gathered from
various sources.

41

basically in place, their proper use and coordination need to be further improved. For instance, reserve requirements for specialized banks and interest rates are still not adjusted in an adequate manner and are therefore ineffective in achieving the desired results. In addition, like central banks everywhere, the PBC remains exceedingly vulnerable to pressures from government agencies for the financing of pet projects and the continuing expectation that banks will automatically meet all their budgetary needs. Moreover, the effectiveness of indirect monetary policy tools is further reduced by the relatively small size of the government security market and by the continued insensitivity to interest rates. Until the basic preconditions for indirect levers to be effective are in place and the policy instruments themselves are perfected, the PBC will likely continue to apply a mixture of direct administrative intervention and indirect policy instruments.

Strengthening the Functions of the Banking System

Reforming the banking system has been proven to be slow and difficult. As far as institutional restructuring is concerned, no fundamental changes have taken place. However, there has been a creation of new banks and an expansion of old ones. Since the PBC has gradually moved toward operating exclusively as a central bank, the commercial banking activities of the PBC have been assigned to other specialized banking institutions. For example, its rural credit activities were transferred to the Agricultural Bank of China, and its urban industrial and commercial credit operations were transferred to the newly created Industrial and Commercial Bank of China (ICBC). The establishment of the ICBC bank relieved the PBC's burden of exercising microfinancial supervision over the nation's public enterprises.

The Construction Bank of China, which was first established in 1954 to manage the fixed capital investment funds, has undergone significant changes since its re-establishment in 1979. Although it is still basically a fiscal agent of the government rather than a bank, its role has changed greatly since the government decided that appropriations for investment funds to enterprises would gradually assume the form of bank loans. Funds for those loans would still come from the budget, but budgetary appropriations would account for a diminishing part of the total fixed-asset investment. The ICBC also extends loans with funds mobilized through mandatory deposits from enterprises. Enterprises intending to carry out fixed-asset investment projects, even with their own funds, must make a prior six-month deposit of funds to be utilized during the following year.

As a major window for China's external financial activities, the BOC took on more responsibility as China's external economic activities expanded rapidly. The BOC's extended business scope now includes international syndicated loans, issuance of foreign currency bonds and other securities, and lending to Sino-foreign joint ventures.

In 1979, China International Trust and Investment Corporation (CITIC), another state-owned financial institution integrating production, technology, finance, and trade, was established, with its main business including: (a) utilizing foreign capital through various forms such as trust deposits and trust investment from foreign countries, direct borrowing from international financial markets, and issuing bonds on foreign capital markets; (b) organizing joint ventures, compensation trade, and other forms of co-production arrangements; and (c) engaging in leasing, real estate business, and consulting services for domestic and foreign clients. Another new bank, the Investment Bank of China (IBC) was set up in 1981 as a specialized bank designated to raise foreign capital for national construction. The bank now operates as an intermediary of both the World Bank and the Asian Development Bank to accept loans and re-lend them to domestic enterprises (Table 3.1).

More important than reorganizing the financial institutions in China is the permission and autonomy given banks to play the role they should in mobilizing and allocating financial resources. To achieve this goal, the decision-making of financial institutions has now been separated from the government administration. Although specialized banks are still basically fiscal agents of the government,

Table 3.1
Major Functions of Financial Institutions in China

The People's Bank

- a. Studying and formulating monetary policy guidelines, decrees and basic rules and regulations on national monetary affairs;

- b. Exercising unified control over currency issuance and regulating currency circulation on the market;

- c. Working out nationwide Credit and Cash Plans;

- d. Organizing, carrying out and bringing about an overall balance of nationwide Credit funds;

- e. Examining and approving the establishment, merger and dissolution of financial institutions;

- f. Exercising unified control over credit and deposit interest rates as well as lending rates in Chinese currency and determining exchange rates between the Chinese currency and foreign currencies;

- g. Controlling and managing foreign exchange and gold reserves;

- h. Coordinating and examining operations of all other financial institutions; and

- i. Operating in the international monetary system on behalf of the Chinese government.

The Agricultural Bank of China

- a. Allocating agricultural funds set aside from fiscal funds of the central government and exercising central controls over various funds for agricultural assistance such as down payment funds for advance product purchase contracts;

- b. Managing the cash resources of various rural enterprise, institutions and non-profit entities;

- c. Handling deposit and lending business in the countryside;

- d. Extending guidance to rural credit associations or cooperatives; and

- e. Guiding the accounting of basic rural economic units.

The Industrial and Commercial Bank of China

- a. Taking in deposits from individuals, enterprises and public service

Table 3.1 (continued)

organizations;

b. Managing working capital funds of state enterprises and providing working capital loans to state, collectively-owned or private enterprises;

c. Managing the technological transformation funds for enterprises and granting loans for the technological transformation of enterprises;

d. Handling the settlement of payments among domestic enterprises; and

e. Managing leasing businesses and economic research.

<u>Bank of China</u>

a. Engaging in all kinds of foreign exchange business and related Chinese currency transactions, mainly including trade and non-trade settlements'

b. Making loans to foreign trade corporations, including foreign currency loans or necessary matching Chinese currency loans and other export credits;

c. Making loans to Sino-foreign joint venture and providing guarantees for financing;

d. Participating in international syndicated loans;

e. Raising funds from international financial market by issuing foreign currency bonds and other securities;

f. Handling foreign currency deposits and remittances; and

g. Signing agreements with foreign governments and central banks, and participating in international financial activities as authorized by the government.

<u>The China International Trust & Investment Corporation</u>

a. Attracting foreign trust deposits and trust investment;

b. Direct borrowing from international financial markets and issuing bonds on foreign capital markets;

c. Organizing joint ventures, compensation trade and processing and assembling arrangements;

d. Engaging in leasing and real estate business; and

e. Providing consulting services for domestic and foreign clients.

Source: Compiled by the authors.

their role has gradually changed. The specialized banks have been given the authority to determine whether or not a proposed project is economically and financially feasible, and are expected to become more independent with respect to credit decisions. Managers of financial institutions are increasingly called upon to make profitability the major criteria in their lending decisions.

Although Chinese banks have more autonomy today than in the past, they are still not responsible for profits and losses. As in many other socialist countries, a significant amount of business activities are not justified on a profit basis alone; rather, business decisions are based on the basis of what the authorities see as needed. Additionally, when the ownership of these specialized banks belongs to the state, which in turn has discretionary power to plan how banks should be operated, profit orientation seems to be unpractical and often in conflict with economic and social goals. With bank profits still being remitted to the state budget, banks have had little freedom or incentive to improve facilities or to increase and upgrade staff in response to the growing demand for better-quality banking services. Furthermore, they have not been expected to show much concern for efficiency and profitability. It is important, therefore, that the enterprise management reforms also be extended to financial institutions.

The Emergence and Growth of Non-Bank Financial Institutions

Over 95 percent of financial sector activities in China are accounted for by the banking system. However, a considerable amount of experimentation in the development of non-bank financial institutions is now underway. Some of these experiments have been started by central or local government authorities, while others appear to have sprung up spontaneously in response to the demand by enterprises for new sources of finance. Currently, non-bank financial institutions include investment and trust companies, leasing companies, pension funds, and insurance companies.

China's trust and investment companies are similar to what are known as finance companies in many other developing countries. They undertake a broad range of lending and investment activities, but cannot accept deposits. Instead, they rely on funds borrowed from other financial institutions or through the issuance of bonds both domestically and internationally. Some 40 such companies had been licensed by the PBC by the beginning of 1991; however, more than 1,000 have been reported in operation at the national and provincial levels.

Leasing began in China in the early 1980s and has developed rapidly over the past few years. Both domestic and foreign leasing is carried out through a number of specialized companies, as well as by the trust and investment companies and, to a lesser extent, by departments of the specialized banks. About a dozen international leasing companies have been licensed, and some 40 domestic leasing companies are reported to be in operation.[6]

Non-bank financial institutions have evolved largely to provide financial services of longer maturity and of greater risks than usually possible for commercial banks. Thus the growth and diversification of financial institutions now taking place in China has been a positive development, enhancing the financial sector's ability to mobilize savings and to direct them efficiently to high-value investment. However, further steps are needed before these institutions can become truly independent, innovative, and competitive entities. Attention must also be given to the regulatory framework within which these institutions are to function.

Of particular importance is the development of contractual savings institutions such as insurance companies, pension funds, and provident funds, which in most countries are second only to the banks as mobilizers of household savings. Contractual savings institutions are stable investors, can take considerable risk, and bring expertise to capital markets. Over time, the growth of pension funds and life insurance could facilitate labor mobility and enterprise efficiency by removing this burden from the current budgets of enterprises.

The Development of Financial Markets

Because China had a highly centralized financial system prior to 1979, the financial market was almost non-existent during the period from 1949 to 1978. However, in the latter part of 1986, the phrase "financial market" or, more precisely "fund market" began to appear in newspapers, and on radio and television. Subsequently, money, bond, and/or other financial markets were gradually established throughout the country.

Money-Market Activities

China's newly developed money market consists of a fully segmented interbank market and a small market for banker's acceptances (BAs) and large-denomination certificates of deposit (CDs). The data on this market are not yet readily available. Therefore, the following discussion is based on information so far released in the press.

Interbank Operations. The development of a money market contributes to the efficiency of the financial sector by allowing financial institutions to transfer surplus funds to other financial institutions instead of directly financing inefficient borrowers or discouraging depositors; and by facilitating the management of bank liabilities through refinancing, thereby increasing the availability of long-term finance for investment. The interbank borrowing market emerged in China when the financial reform put pressure on the banks to use their funds more efficiently. Under the old system, the head office of a bank (at that time, it was mainly the PBC) allocated the loanable funds to different branches according to the need projected in that area. Branches only needed to disburse the loan according to the head office's instructions. They had hardly any incentive or leeway to expand their business. The reform has called for changing this practice, which means that branches are now given only part of funds for loans and their business depends on the attraction of deposits and temporary borrowing from other banks.

A very important characteristic of China's interbank borrowing market is that it is not only a market for overnight loans to cover the positions of banks, but also a means of covering temporary shortages of loanable funds. For example, in February of a given year, a branch of the Agricultural Bank of China decided to disperse a loan to an enterprise in May of the same year. Due to the lack of other instruments, particularly short-term instruments in which to invest the temporary surplus funds, the idea arose to find another bank that had a chance to make a loan but needed temporary funding for their loan. As a result of this practice, the concept of interbank borrowing was modified substantially. The interbank market has become a fairly "long" short-term lending and borrowing between banks to make the use of their loanable funds more efficient. Sometimes the maturity of interbank borrowing in China can be as long as 365 days, though this is not the case for the majority of interbank borrowing.

The central bank imposes no restrictions on the interest rates on interbank borrowing in the same sector. The interest rates of interbank borrowing are determined through consultation between lenders and borrowers. Generally speaking, they are slightly lower than interest rates for working capital loans. The main reason is that the purpose of lending money to banks in the same sector (i.e., an ABC branch to another ABC branch) is not to make money but to support each office of the same specialized bank. The interest rate for loans outside the sector is higher than that inside the sector. However, the margin in upward fluctuation is less than 20 percent in most cases.[7]

The structure of the banking system also influences the role and size of the interbank borrowing market in China. At present, interbank borrowing mainly takes the following forms: (a) interbank borrowing market with the PBC as the center and other specialized banks as the main body that integrates activities in cities and rural areas; (b) joint interbank borrowing in urban areas led by the IBC branches; (c) the rural market organized by the ABC with the participation of rural credit cooperatives; and (d) a financial network set up voluntarily by banks in several big and me-

dium-sized cities to form a regional market. The interbank borrowing can be graded into three vertical levels: provincial, city, and
national. Horizontally, many inter-sector, inter-province, and inter-
city networks have been formed.

Table 3.2 is a report on interbank borrowing activities published
in a Chinese newspaper, *Financial Times*, on July 16, 1988. Other
newspapers, such as *Economic Daily* and *Beijing Daily*, often carry
similar reports. By examining the information given in the report,
one can grasp the basic characteristics of the interbank borrowing
market in China. The first column of the table lists the names of
different money centers, usually geographical names representing
the horizontal network voluntarily set up by several major cities.
The Chongqing network, for example, has established business
relationships with 24 provinces, including 70 cities and 140
branches of different banks. The second column shows the date the
transactions were conducted. The third and fourth columns indicate the amount of funds they planned to lend and borrow. Column
5 shows the number of deals concluded. The actual amount of
transactions concluded on that day or in the period of time is listed
in Column 6. If the planned amount of funds to be lent and
borrowed equals the amount of the actual transactions concluded,
then every participant on that day has successfully made a deal,
but usually this is not the case. The amount of borrowing is
typically larger than that of lending.

Column 7 shows the maturity of the borrowed funds, including
the longest and shortest maturities. As previously indicated, the
maturity of interbank borrowing in China can be as long as 365
days. The shortest maturity is about three days. According to a
survey done on 11 money centers, a maturity of seven days
accounted for 7.5 percent of the total number of transactions. A
maturity of eight days to 30 days accounted for the bulk of
transactions—48 percent, while a maturity of one to three months
accounted for 29.6 percent. Only a very small percentage is taken
by maturities of six to twelve months long. Based on the volume
of transactions, the maturities within seven days, between eight

Table 3.2
Interbank Market Activities Reports

Name of the market rates	Transaction date	Funds available		Number of deals concluded	Total amount of transactions	Maturity		Lowest	Highest rates	Average rates
		To lend	To borrow			Longest	Shortest			
Beijing	7.10	28,300	25,300	14	29,300	90	7	5.4	5.79	5.4
Shanghai	7.9	24,850	8,550	8	14,050	31	10	5.55	5.7	5.66
Guangzhou	7.6-7.12	1,007,750	61,600	4	3,700	365	60	5.85	9.0	6.29
Shenyang	6.29-7.4	3,200	2,700	8	5,400	93	60	5.88	6.0	5.97
Wuhan	7.10	6,300	2,150	9	7,900	90	20	5.55	6.03	5.75
Chongqing	7.6-7.10	26,500	25,500	14	15,100	90	3	5.64	6.0	5.85
Shantou	7.9	1,500	1,800	2	1,500	90	60	5.85	5.85	5.85
Nanjing	7.6-7.11	13,800	15,000	7	13,800	92	18	5.7	6.0	5.87
Taiyuan	7.9	4,000	4,000	1	2,000	20	20	5.5	5.55	5.55
Hangzhou	7.7-7.13	8,850	9,580	9	8,350	92	11	5.7	5.85	5.73

Sources: Financial Times, Beijing, China (July 16, 1988).

days to three months, and three months to six months accounted for 11.2 percent, 72.1 percent and 14.3 percent, respectively.[8]

Columns 8, 9, and 10 show the interest rates at which transactions are concluded (high, low, and average respectively). The fluctuations of interest rates are very narrow, between 5.5 percent and 6.5 percent, as compared to those of interbank borrowing markets in other countries due to the reasons explained above. They do not reflect the overall supply and demand of credit in the market.

Although the interbank borrowing market is still small and is unevenly developed in the different geographical areas, it is a very important development in China's financial sector. A robust interbank money market would greatly facilitate the liquidity management of the specialized banks and would achieve a more efficient use of financial resources through horizontal flows from areas of limited demand to areas with high-priority needs. Interbank borrowing provides the central bank with signals that can assist it in setting deposit and lending rates at more appropriate levels and offers a stronger institutional base for the execution of the central bank's monetary policy. It is expected that this development will soon be followed by the introduction of other short-term financial instrument markets such as bank bills and commercial papers.

Banker's Acceptance and Certificates of Deposit. The first banker's acceptance (BA) transaction since the founding of the People's Republic of China was conducted by a bank in Shanghai in February 1981. After the initial experiments in Shanghai, this operation spread quickly to other cities. In April 1985 the central bank decided that BA transactions would become the standard business of all banks.

Any state-owned or collective-owned industrial and commercial enterprise or joint venture that enjoys the status of a legal entity and has proper commodity transactions can issue papers that can be accepted by banks. The scope of BAs has gradually been expanding. At first they were limited to the sales of seasonal commodities and to sales with deferred payment. As a result of this new business, sale transactions between enterprises have developed from the old form of delivery against payment to that of sale on credit. The increasing use of BAs has brought another credit instrument to China's money market and has promoted business activities and tapped financial resources.

The interest rates for a discount of a BA are in line with the rate for working capital loans the bank provides to enterprises. If banks need cash, they can rediscount the draft with the central bank. When conditions warrant, a secondary market for banker's acceptance is expected to be opened.

Large certificates of deposit (CDs) have been utilized to a very limited extent. Only a small number of enterprises and financial institutions are allowed to issue these certificates. These CDs are denominated in 10,000 to 100,000 yuan to attract funds solely from institutional depositors. The maturities of these certificates are within one year. Interest rates are slightly higher than bank deposits of the same maturity. CDs are the only type of short-term investment instruments available other than demand deposit for entities.

Capital Market Development

China's capital market for long-term bonds and quasi-equity shares has developed fairly rapidly since its commencement in 1986. However, funds raised through the market account for only a fraction of total financing.[9] Bank credit is still a major source of financing for the nation's investment activities. A more detailed analysis of capital markets, including bonds and stocks, is provided in the following chapters.

In conclusion, the major objective of a financial system is to contribute to rapid, efficient, stable, and equitable growth. Toward this end, China's reform efforts have focused on the efficiency of the financial system by improving competition, market orientation, and innovation. Although China has taken preliminary steps in these areas, qualitative changes have not been attained. China's financial system remains primitive and financial reforms incomplete. Qualitative changes can only be achieved after comprehensive reform of the financial system is accomplished, in which all factors affecting an efficient financial system are put in place.

If the developments in these areas indeed take place, it is likely that the Chinese financial system will look dramatically different in the next decade. In terms of financial institutions, banks may lose their present dominance, with their market share declining from its current 95 percent to a much lower percentage, assuming an increased role for insurance companies, pension funds, and other non-bank financial institutions, such as trust and investment companies, leasing companies, and investment funds.

The breakdown of instruments or financial assets may also be quite different. Looking to the future, the rising income, the changes foreseen in enterprises and household financial management, the growing volume and variety of financial instruments available, and the greater openness of the economy to foreign trade and investment will all affect the amounts and forms of financial assets that individuals and institutions may choose to hold.

The establishment of conditions necessary for efficient and decentralized investment decisions is somewhat more complicated than those for production decisions because of the long-term nature of the former's consequences and the likelihood that those consequences may lie beyond the time horizon of responsible decision-makers. Lack of clear definition of creditors' rights and debtors' responsibilities makes banks and enterprises unable to realize independent management and self-restraint. Imperfections in the current system still lead to the irrational behavior of both. While decentralization can result in more efficient resource use, it complicates the task of managing aggregate demand and requires the development of quite different policy tools and instruments, better and more timely information flows to the policy-makers, and new techniques of analysis and policy planning.

Financial reform will also require new attitudes and skills. Massive training of regulatory authorities, bankers, and financial market participants has just begun and is expected to be an area of major focus for the coming decade. At the same time, the physical systems for the delivery of financial systems are expected to improve. In this regard, computerization and communication between various financial institutions and markets, as well as between markets/institutions and the regulatory authority, will be of crucial importance. Because China is making a drastic change, it has the great advantage of not being saddled with past habits and traditions. Just as countries whose plants and machinery were destroyed by the Second World War were able to rebuild a modern industry, China may leapfrog developments to a new, modern financial system. At a later stage of the reform, the innovation and transfer of international financial technology should be promoted.

NOTES

1. The budget needs no explanation. The credit plan sets out the expected sources and uses of banking funds. The cash plan specifies the planned change in currency in circulation as a net result of cash transactions between the government sector (including enterprises) and the household and farm sectors.

2. A good discussion on defects of direct controls over monetary policy can be found in Paul Volcker, Miguel Mancera, and Jean Godeaux, *Perspectives on the Role of a Central Bank*, International Monetary Fund, 1991.

3. These banks performed specific functions or served specific sectors. For example, the ABC served the agricultural sector. The CBC allocated government investment funds to specific projects and enterprises. The BOC acted as China's "external window," specializing in foreign exchange transactions and the settlement of international trade accounts, as well as engaging in international borrowing activities. The responsibility of the PIC was to provide insurance policies to cover marine risk that might occur in international trade activities.

4. See Paul Volcker, Miguel Mancera, and Jean Godeaux, *Perspectives on the Role of a Central Bank*.

5. Please notice that individual and entity investors were treated differently before 1988. The rates were usually two to three percentage points lower for institutional depositors.

6. World Bank, *China Finance and Investment* (Washington, D.C., March 1987), 66.

7. Ibid.

    8. Bin Xia, *China's Financial Markets in the Making* (Beijing: China Youth Publication Company, 1987), 32.
    9. Ibid.

4

The Emergence of the
Securities Market

FACTORS AFFECTING THE EMERGENCE OF
THE SECURITIES MARKET

Since 1978, China has embarked on a complex and difficult process of economic reforms. Part of this complexity is derived from the essential inter-relatedness of the many facets of the economy, and consequently, the success of one facet is dependent on the progress achieved in the others. However, there are two major changes in China's economic system that are believed to have stimulated the emergence of its securities market.[1]

Decentralization and Rationalization of Investment Activities

The replacement of budgetary capital grants by interest-bearing loans and the frequent adjustments in interest rates that reflect market developments have been the most important measures taken by the government to improve the efficiency of financial resource allocation. At present, the government no longer assumes the entire risk for poor investment projects and negative rates of return. The share of economic activity covered by mandatory production and investment allocation has been dramatically reduced. The share of government budget-financed investment of

China's total investment also has dropped considerably; therefore, the direct role of the government in savings and investment has declined markedly. At the same time, the share of enterprise and local government savings, reflecting the retention of earnings, has increased substantially.

The decentralization of investment decisions has given rise to the need for an efficient system of financial intermediation. In particular, decentralized enterprises lack both the resources and means to determine the most efficient investment in the economy as a whole. Individual households are even less expert in decisions such as where to invest their savings. Therefore, the need to create financial intermediation between savers and investors has become urgent.

Increase in Financial Autonomy of Enterprises

Decentralization of decision-making authority over production for enterprises has logically led to the decentralization of control over financial resources. Enterprises have been made to rely increasingly on internally generated resources and on the financial system rather than on the fiscal budget for funding their investments. In this environment, new financial markets and instruments are needed and skillful financial management is crucial to an enterprise's success.

Along with the economic reform, a large number of enterprises have been established and expanded, further fueling the demand for funds. Therefore, as the economic reform deepens, the sustained growth and stability of these enterprises will depend increasingly on the availability of new sources of financing. These changes have been essential to the emergence and development of new financial markets.

THE SCOPE OF THE SECURITIES MARKET

China's securities market currently consists of a wide range of financial instruments, including government bonds or treasury bonds; index bonds; municipal government bonds; and bonds issued by state-owned specialized banks, non-bank financial institutions, and large industrial enterprises. Stock issuance is permitted for some selected state-owned enterprises, all collectively-owned and private firms.

Government bonds started to float in 1981, primarily to finance the government budget deficit. They were mainly purchased by state and collectively owned enterprises and local governments, as well as private firms, and individuals. Initial sales in the early 1980s were mostly on an involuntary basis. The quota for purchase by each enterprise was based on the enterprise's after-tax profits or cash situation. Purchase by individuals was first encouraged in 1982, and recently accounted for over half of the government bonds sold.

Since 1985, two significant measures were introduced to enhance the attractiveness of government bonds. First, maturities have shortened substantially. In the early 1980s, bonds carried a maximum maturity of ten years; in the mid-1980s, the average maturity was reduced to five years; and toward the end of the decade, the maturity was further reduced to three years. Second, interest rates of government bonds have been progressively increased. The early issues (through 1984) only carried rates of 4 percent for institutional investors (mostly enterprises) and 8 percent for individuals (households). In 1985, both interest rates were raised by 1 percent and subsequently they were adjusted upward several times. By 1990 the interest rate for institutional investors had increased from 5 percent to 10 percent, while that for households had increased to 14 percent. Despite upward adjustments in interest rates on government bonds, the rates remained well below those paid on time deposits of similar maturities.

There have also been changes in the methods through which government bonds are sold. Prior to 1991 government bonds were sold exclusively through government committees, which arranged mandatory purchases by institutions and individuals. Starting in 1991, however, selected government bonds were floated through an underwriting system whereby a group of investment and trust companies would float the bonds in the market. In April 1991, for example, some 2.5 billion yuan of treasury bonds were issued through an underwriting syndicate for the first time.[2] Although the financial markets are still relatively undeveloped, a limited amount of secondary trading has been permitted for some bonds. Initially, government bonds could only be discounted by the People's Bank of China or its branches. Later, bonds held by individuals became negotiable and enterprises were allowed to use bond holdings as collateral for obtaining financing, mostly in the form of loan.

A special issue of *indexed bonds* was made available to households in 1989 to meet the particularly large financing needs of the government. Their maturity was three years, and the coupon rate was 1 percent above an inflation "allowance." In addition, there have also been several special issues for development purposes. These include the state key construction bonds (1987 and 1988) and special state bonds issued in 1989.

Specialized banks began to issue *financial bonds* to individuals in 1985 as one of the results of the financial reforms in which the distribution of funds between the central bank and the various specialized banks was changed to one of lending and borrowing. Specialized banks were allowed to supplement their loanable funds by improving their services to attract more deposits, by borrowing from the central bank, or by issuing financial instruments such as CDs and bonds. Non-bank financial institutions, such as trust and investment companies, were also allowed to issue bonds to finance their special investment projects. These were often large infrastructure projects or projects with advanced technology that were introduced with some foreign capital.

Some large state enterprises began issuing *enterprise bonds* in 1987. They were large electrical, metallurgical, nonferrous, and petrochemical enterprises that often required large amounts of investment. *Construction bonds* were also issued in 1988 and 1989 to finance the large construction of manufacturing facilities or transportation facilities. These enterprises issued bonds or stocks mainly because investment funds from budgetary allocations were substantially reduced as a result of financial reforms. Moreover, many newly established small-scale enterprises were not even eligible for such allocations from the government. To start up an investment, or to expand their operations, enterprises had to seek alternative ways to raise funds.

The issuing of bonds and stocks to raise funds was first authorized as an experiment in a few cities, namely Shenyang, Shanghai, and the Guangdong province, and was later expanded to Beijing, Chongqing, Xiamen, and other large cities. These areas were chosen because of the need for enterprises in these cities to take the initiative to raise capital. Shenyang, the capital city of the Liaoning province, is an important industrial base in Northern China. Shanghai, which 40 years ago housed a stock exchange more influential and international in scope than Hong Kong's, is China's most important industrial and commercial city. Guangdong province, abundant with tropical resources and adjacent to Hong Kong, has seen its industrial and commercial activities expand tremendously since 1979. Guangdong province has been in the forefront of China's overall economic reform and has aggressively taken major reform measures to liberalize its economy and open its trade and investment to the rest of the world. However, all these areas faced a common problem: they needed to raise a substantial amount of funds to finance infrastructural development necessitated by the rapid increases in investment projects as well as to enhance their investment funding levels during the time that the government was reforming the fund allocation system under which the budgetary allocations of investment funds to enterprises were greatly reduced.

Table 4.1 shows the total outstanding financial instruments and their relative importance in the financial markets. As expected, government bonds account for a majority share of total securities issued during the period surveyed. At the same time, corporate bonds (by state-owned, collectively owned, and private enterprises) were also a major financial instrument in the Chinese market.

Households, as indicated in Figure 4.1, were the main holders of government bonds, accounting for about half of the total bonds issued. Enterprises held about one-third of the same security while banks and non-bank financial institutions took the rest of the

Table 4.1
Total Outstanding of Financial Instruments, 1981–90
(in billions of yuan)

	Amount issued	Percent of total	Amount outstanding	Percent of total
Government bonds	57.0	35.7	42.0	32.5
Financial bonds	30.0	18.8	25.0	19.4
Construction bonds	8.6	5.4	8.6	6.7
Corporate bonds	37.5	23.5	27.0	20.9
Other bonds	22.0	13.8	22.0	17.0
Stocks	4.5	2.8	4.5	3.5
Total	159.6	100.0	129.1	100.0

Source: Data gathered from various sources.

holdings. For other government bonds (construction, indexed, and other special state bonds), enterprises and households held roughly the same importance (Figure 4.2).

Bonds and stocks issued by enterprises, rather than those issued by the government or financial institutions, will be discussed in later chapters since the former type of securities tend to have a more significant impact on China's economic structure. Besides offering new vehicles for mobilizing funds, financing through corporate bonds and stocks may pressure enterprises to improve management, enhance efficiency and competitiveness, and achieve better financial performance. It thus has significant implications for China's financial system and the economy as a whole.

ENVIRONMENT AND REGULATORY FRAMEWORK

For a country with a large centrally planned economy, and without a financial market for several decades, the concept of

Figure 4.1
Issues of Government Bonds by Holders, 1981–90
(in billions of yuan)

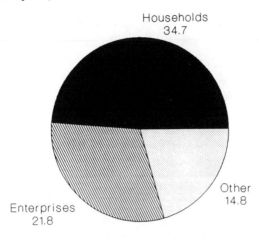

Households
34.7

Other
14.8

Enterprises
21.8

Treasury bonds

Source: Information gathered from
various sources.

bonds or stocks could not be fully understood by either issuers or investors during the early stages of the securities market development. Evidently there were no guidelines for them to follow and it was impossible to copy the market practices of other countries without substantial modifications to suit China's economic and political conditions. Therefore, the experiment with bond and stock issues was carried out on a trial and error basis, attempting to put Western financing techniques to work in a still largely regulated economy. As a result, during the early stages the bonds and stocks issued by enterprises were of a variety of types with many unique characteristics, reflecting the environment in which they operated.

Figure 4.2
Issues of Other Government Bonds by Holders, 1981–90
(in billions of yuan)

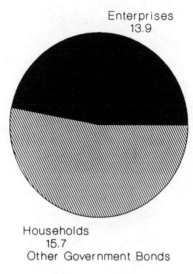

Enterprises
13.9

Households
15.7
Other Government Bonds

Source: Information gathered from
various sources.

As more securities were issued, securities regulations began to merge. In the last quarter of 1986, local regulations on stocks and bonds in Beijing, Guangdong province, and the Xiamen special economic zone were promulgated. The focus of these early regulations was basically to define the concept of stocks and bonds, the businesses that were eligible for issuing securities, the conditions and procedures under which securities could be issued, the principles for the purchase and transfer of the securities, and the guidelines for the distribution of dividends and interest payments. The regulatory pattern was similar but not identical in each city or region.

A national regulation was not promulgated until the State Council, the highest government administrative organ, issued a circular on the administration of securities along with the Interim Regulations Governing the Issuance of Bonds for State-owned Enterprises on March 27, 1987. The new rules promulgated by the State Council in some respect departed from earlier regional regulations and underscored the difficult task the government had to face in the process of financial reform: how to strike a balance between the financial freedom of enterprise and the state's need for overall control. The circular recognized the positive role of securities in activating financial markets, resolving shortages of capital, and promoting economic cooperation among enterprises. It also recognized the problems caused by a lack of uniform administration, control, and regulatory framework. With the publication of the State Council's regulations, it became clear that the government wanted the experimentation of bond and stock issuing to continue, but on a more carefully supervised basis. Any local provisions that conflicted with the new regulations issued by the State Council were to be amended and recorded with the Central Bank (Appendix III).

The new national regulations authorized only bond issues and not the issuance of stocks by the state-owned enterprises. The right to issue stocks was still limited, in general, to a small number of collective-owned and private enterprises. With very few exceptions, state-owned enterprises were not allowed to issue stocks to the public.

Based on these regulations, it became apparent that government policy regarding the securities market was more oriented toward solving short-term problems than encouraging long-term development of the market. Restrictions on the use of proceeds and on interest rates enterprises could offer, for example, prohibited a rapid and healthy development of the market. The regulatory framework lacked other important elements such as a law defining the nature of a limited company, the disclosure requirements, and the auditing standards, each essential to a well-functioning market.

For the time being, the regulating and administrating agency for the securities market in China remains the Central Bank, which also authorizes its local branches to approve applications for securities issuance within the provinces or cities where they are located. The reason the Central Bank rather than an independent regulatory agency assumed the responsibility of regulating security issuing activities is that the government wants the Central Bank to control and coordinate the overall flow of investment funds and investment needs, including investment financed by issuing securities. The government is particularly concerned that: (a) investments and other expenditures financed by the sale of these instruments can cause excessive domestic demand; (b) the new financial instruments can draw funds out of the banking system; (c) the resources mobilized through these instruments can be used for wasteful purposes; and (d) enterprises can exceed their capacities for serving debt and thus get into unnecessary and socially costly financial difficulties. Consequently, the government attempts to eliminate all the possible negative elements that may be associated with the securities and retains control over the economy. Local branches of the Central Bank are mainly responsible for implementing the national policy according to local conditions, approving applications, and monitoring the securities market development in their respective areas.

Since the publication of the State Council regulations, the Central Bank and other financial agencies of various local governments have issued a number of regulations concerning the examination, approval, and establishment of financial intermediate institutions that will be engaged in securities dealing activities. One such regulation calls for the establishment of a licensing system for securities exchange and stipulates that only licensed financial entities can engage in the brokerage business. Local regulations have also established procedures for the entry of financial instruments into the market, the conduct of market participants, and the deployment of counters for securities exchanges. The Shanghai authorities have promulgated several regulations regarding the issue of securities by enterprises in the Shanghai region and the establishment and operations of the Shanghai exchange market.

New legislation to help shape the basic legal framework is currently being drafted. The People's Bank is working on "Procedures Concerning the Issuance of Bonds and the Provisional

Procedures for the Distribution of Stocks" and "Rules for Exchanges in Negotiable Securities" that will govern securities issuing and trading activities throughout the country. The government of Shanghai and Shenzhen have also increased their work on drafting local bylaws in this regard. All these legislations will set comprehensive provisions for the management of the securities market.

NOTES

1. World Bank, *China Finance and Investment* (Washington, D.C., March, 1987), 4.

2. Hoe Ge Khor, "China—Macroeconomic Cycles in the 1980s," *IMF Working Paper*, WP/91/85, 1991, 21.

Securities Market Participants

Because the securities market in China is still in its very early stage of development, and individuals are limited in securities dealings, the security market at present is largely dominated by enterprises that serve both as issuers and investors. Before discussing each type of market participant, it is important to understand the different types of business enterprises that are operating in the Chinese economy.

TYPES OF BUSINESS ENTERPRISES

The Chinese economy consists of a very large number of business enterprises, although most of them are small in size. The number of industrial enterprises alone amounts to nearly half a million. In terms of number, only a small fraction of business enterprises are organized under state ownership. Other forms of ownership and operation include collectively owned, private enterprises, joint-stock companies, and foreign investment enterprises. Table 5.1 indicates the importance of each type of enterprise in the Chinese economy.

State-owned Enterprises

Although state-owned enterprises account for only 4 percent of the total number of industrial enterprises in China, they play a

Table 5.1
Gross Value of Industrial Output by Enterprises, 1978–88

	1978	1979	1980	1981	1982	1983	1984	1985	1986	1987	1988
					(In billions of yuan)						
Total	423.7	468.2	515.5	540.0	581.1	646.0	761.8	971.6	1119.4	1381.3	1822.4
State-owned	328.9	367.4	391.6	403.7	432.6	473.9	526.3	630.2	697.1	825.0	1035.1
Collectively-owned	94.8	100.8	121.3	132.9	144.2	166.3	226.3	311.7	375.2	478.2	658.7
Individually owned	0.0	0.0	2.5	3.3	4.3	5.8	9.2	29.7	47.2	78.1	128.6
					(In percent of total)						
State-owned	77.6	78.5	76.0	74.8	74.4	73.4	69.1	64.9	62.3	59.7	56.8
Collectively-owned	22.4	21.5	23.5	24.6	24.8	25.7	29.7	32.1	33.5	34.6	36.1
Individually owned	0.0	0.0	0.5	0.6	0.7	0.9	1.2	3.1	4.2	5.7	7.1

Source: Statistical Yearbook of China, State Statistical Bureau, China (1989), p. 225.

significant role in the economy. Usually large state-owned enterprises are under the supervision of industrial ministries in Beijing, mostly operating in the manufacturing sector. Yearly production quotas, procurement, and financial planning are basically established between the ministries and enterprises themselves. In recent years the enterprises have also been allowed to produce other goods in addition to those specified by the ministries. At the same time, they are also allowed to handle some marketing and financial matters by themselves.

Medium- and small-sized state-owned enterprises can either be owned by the central government or local governments, or jointly owned. It appears that these enterprises have greater autonomy in decision making and are more active in the securities market. In 1989 there were about 10,000 large state-owned enterprises, whereas the medium- and small-sized enterprises numbered over 80,000.

Collectively Owned Enterprises

Collectively owned enterprises can be more accurately described as semi-private and semi–state-owned enterprises. These enterprises consist largely of partnerships, under which individual partners raise their own funds and work together. However, many of these collective enterprises were reorganized as semi–state-owned enterprises in the late 1950s and early 1960s. In so doing, the members' or employees' proprietary rights to the means of production were partly or totally bought by local governments. During the 1960s and 1970s, most of the larger urban industrial collectives were placed under the direct control of the national and provincial bureaucracies.

The industrial reform that took place in the mid-1980s has greatly affected these collectively owned enterprises. As a result of the reforms, the government's control over these enterprises and its role in providing funding has substantially diminished, thus enhancing the autonomy of the enterprises' management markedly. However, the relative autonomy of collectively owned enterprises made possible through the reforms is not necessarily an advantage to them: collectives today are facing increasing competition for raw materials, production inputs, and funds from state-owned enterprises.

Private Enterprises

Although China nationalized most of its private enterprises in the early 1950s, some of them, mostly very small in size, were able to survive and continue to operate in the economy. These enterprises were located mainly in the service sector in the eastern and southern parts of China. Typical private businesses include barber shops, tailor shops, restaurants, and street vendors and require a minimum of start-up capital and operate completely outside the state planning system.

Although the number of individual enterprises steadily declined in the 1970s, owing to the adverse effect of the Cultural Revolution, they rebounded sharply in the 1980s with the numbers reaching over six million by the end of 1989. More than 90 percent of these enterprises are in rural areas, with many employing a very small number of workers. Private firms that employ 100 to 1,000 workers account for less than 1 percent of the total number of private-owned enterprises.

Joint-stock Enterprises

Joint-stock enterprises are a new form of business in China. They are established by several enterprises pooling their capital and other resources together in order to start a new business or to expand existing operations. Joint-stock enterprises can be formed by state-owned enterprises or collectively owned enterprises, or between state-owned and collectively owned enterprises. They can also issue stocks to outside investors to raise funds for their operations.

Compared with collectively owned and private-owned enterprises, joint-stock enterprises pose the greatest challenge yet to the state ownership system since the classification of this type of enterprise as either state, collective, or private becomes extremely difficult. For example, when the Beijing Tianqiao Department Store Company first issued stocks to the public in 1984, following the merger of two department stores and a wholesale store, it faced an ownership identity problem. The company sold 51 percent of its shares to the government, 26 percent to banks, 20 percent to other enterprises, and 3 percent to individuals. Consequently, when it came time for the company to register, it was not sure what type of ownership it should claim and what type of company it should be declared.

However, joint-stock enterprises are a new development and remain very much at the experimental stage. They do not operate and function exactly like a share-holding company in other countries. The formation of this type of company, the scale of its operation, and the direction of investment are still heavily influenced by the government; shareholders only have limited power in the enterprise's decision making.

Foreign Investment Enterprises

Foreign investment enterprises have grown rapidly since 1979, when China passed the Foreign Investment Law allowing the participation of foreign investment in its economy.[1] By the end of 1991, over 20,000 joint ventures between Chinese enterprises and foreign companies were established, involving foreign investment of more than U.S. $30 billion.

Most of these enterprises have taken the form of joint ventures— enterprises jointly owned by foreigners and PRC entities. There are two types of joint ventures currently operating in China: equity and contractual joint ventures. Under the arrangements of the former, both foreign and Chinese companies are responsible for the venture's operations and profits are shared based on the equity contribution of each partner. In the latter form of joint ventures, however, partners share the profits according to agreed-upon terms prior to production rather than according to their respective equity shares.[2]

More recently, many foreign companies have established wholly foreign-owned enterprises in China. The main advantage of this type of enterprise for foreign investors is that they have flexibility in managing the enterprise. However, the foreign investor is solely responsible for the risks, gains, or losses of the operation.

Although the total production of foreign investment enterprises is still small compared to that of state-owned enterprises, these enterprises play a catalytic role in promoting change for other Chinese firms. Joint ventures mostly adopt a Western management style and are profit-oriented, with autonomy in areas such as operations, marketing, and financing.

SECURITIES MARKET PARTICIPANTS

Since information regarding the enterprises that have partici-pated in securities issuing activities is not publicly available, the discussion in this section is primarily based on the survey and field interview by the authors.

Size of issuing enterprises. The survey results indicate that securities issuing enterprises varied greatly in size, judging either by the number of employees or by total assets. It was also found that some issuers were very small private firms while others were large state-owned enterprises. The mean of the number of employ-ees of issuing enterprises in the survey sample was 877. Moreover, the size of the total assets of the securities issuers also varied widely; small issuers were represented by collectively and private-owned enterprises while large ones were basically state-owned enterprises.

Types of businesses. The survey also indicates that securities issuers were engaged in various types of businesses, with a heavy concentration in the light industrial and services sectors (Figure 5.1). A small number of issuers were from high-technology and heavy industries. It appears that securities issued by enterprises in the services sector were more attractive because investment in this sector tended to be small and cash flows could be quickly gener-ated.

Figure 5.1
Line of Business of Securities Issuers (in percent of respondents)

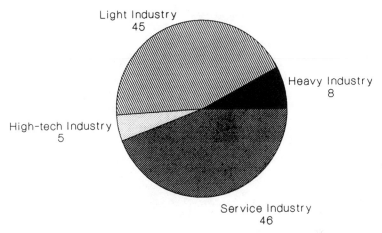

Light Industry
45

Heavy Industry
8

High-tech Industry
5

Service Industry
46

Source: Survey by the authors.

Forms of ownership. As far as the type of ownership is concerned, about one-third of the issuers in the survey reported that they were state-owned and over two-thirds were collectives. Private-owned and other types of enterprises were of minor importance, only accounting for about 3 percent of total issuers (Figure 5.2). However, there were some differences between bond and stock issuers. Bond issuers were mostly state-owned enterprises, whereas stock issuers were largely collectives. Newly established enterprises (with operating histories of five years or shorter) were major players in the market, accounting for over 40 percent of total issues indicated in the survey (Figure 5.3). This demonstrates that raising capital from the securities market has now become a significant source of financing for young companies.

Financial position. Most of the issuers indicated that they were financially sound enterprises. Over 70 percent of the respondents said that they had been experiencing a rapid increase in operations and profits in the past five years (Figure 5.4). It is not surprising

Figure 5.2
Forms of Ownership of Securities Issuers (in percent of respondents)

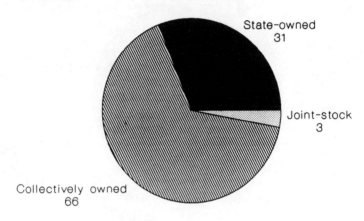

State-owned
31

Joint-stock
3

Collectively owned
66

Source: Survey by the Authors.

that, at this initial stage, the financial soundness of the issuers is the most important factor as virtually no legal protection is available for investors. Furthermore, there are no other supporting institutions, such as credit rating agencies, to assist in evaluating the securities. Because of this, the central bank carefully reviews the operational history of the issuers, making sure that they have been profitable.

It should be stressed that in China's current economic environment, profitable enterprises are not necessarily efficient and competitive. Due to the incompleteness of the industrial reform in general and of price reform in particular, the enterprises with certain production lines, particularly consumer products, are more profitable than others, such as those in heavy industries. However, these profitable enterprises may have to face more competition as the reforms deepen. The emergence of new firms, the shift of

Figure 5.3
Number of Years in Operation (in percent of respondents)

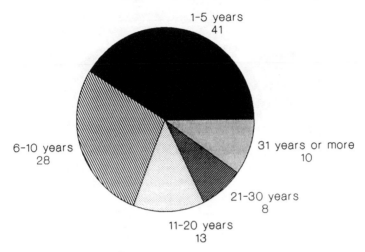

Source: Survey by the Authors.

production capacity from other sources, and the rapidly increasing number of foreign enterprises can all alter the present monopolist position of many Chinese firms. Until then, they will have to adjust themselves to market changes in order to maintain their competitiveness in the marketplace.

Sources of financing. The survey also confirms that the government budgetary allocation of investment funds to state-owned enterprises has declined in the past few years. In fact, the majority of collectives could hardly obtain any form of government funding for their operations. Bank loans, while becoming a more important source of enterprise financing, remained far from adequate in terms of meeting the overall financing needs of enterprises. Hence, the option of raising funds through issuance of bonds and stocks became increasingly important, particularly for the collectives. Nevertheless, funds raised through the securities market remained rather small, accounting for only about 5 percent of the total financing needs of the issuing enterprises (Figure 5.5).

Figure 5.4
Financial Performance of Securities Issuers

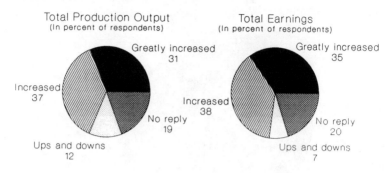

Total Production Output
(In percent of respondents)

Greatly increased
31

Increased
37

No reply
19

Ups and downs
12

Total Earnings
(In percent of respondents)

Greatly increased
35

Increased
38

No reply
20

Ups and downs
7

Source: Survey by the Authors.

Figure 5.5
Sources of Funds of Securities Issuers (in percent)

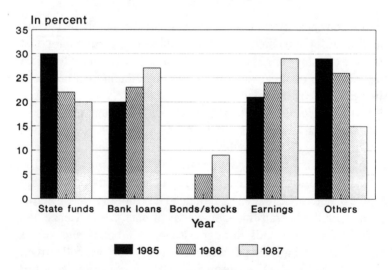

In percent

35
30
25
20
15
10
5
0

State funds   Bank loans   Bonds/stocks   Earnings   Others

Year

■ 1985   ▨ 1986   □ 1987

Source: Survey by the Authors.

The need for funds. The survey revealed that most enterprises that had issued securities during the period studied were still in urgent need of funds. When asked whether they felt it was urgent to raise funds through the securities market, about one-quarter of respondents reported "very urgent" and over two-thirds replied "urgent," while only a small fraction of respondents said "no." This finding illustrates the declining importance of government-sponsored funds and the increasing need for funds from other sources.

The above results from the authors' survey indicate that, although the securities market is presently small in China and the number of market participants is limited, its potential appears to be great. This is reflected in the fact that a majority of market participants felt that they had no other option but to issue securities to meet their financing needs. Most importantly, as the reform process continues, the financial environment will change dramatically. As the private sector assumes greater power in the economy, the role of the government will be diminished. At that time, enterprises will have to compete for funds and the securities market will rise rapidly in importance.

NOTES

1. See Phillip D. Grub and Jian Hai Lin, *Foreign Direct Investment in China* (Westport, Conn.: Quorum Books, 1991), for greater detail.

2. A good discussion on different forms of foreign operations in China is provided in Grub and Lin, *Foreign Direct Investment In China*, 61-77.

6

Bond Issuing Activities

Before the Chinese government issued the Interim Regulations for the Administration of Enterprise Bonds in March 1987, enterprises were free of restrictions in choosing either bonds or stocks as a means to raise funds. After the regulations were enacted, enterprises had to comply with the new rules, which were regarded as an attempt to tighten control over the development of the securities market by the government. The government's argument was that, in order to facilitate the transformation of state-owned enterprises into other forms of enterprises and to avoid the complications of the ownership identity issues, state-owned enterprises should not be allowed to issue stocks. Instead, they could only issue bonds to raise funds, which could be backed up by the assets invested by the government as collateral. On the other hand, collectively owned enterprises would be encouraged to issue stocks rather than bonds, as investors could hardly be protected for their investment if their bonds were to default.

Before discussing the survey results regarding bond issuing activities, the ownership of the issuing enterprises in the primary bonds market must be noted since ownership status entitles the enterprise to different conditions under which they can issue securities. Consequently, their behavior and responses to the market may be different. In this survey, about 80 percent of the bond issuers were state-owned enterprises and the rest were either collectively owned or joint-stock enterprises. This distinction is essential in order to understand the way in which the survey results are presented in this and following chapters.

SURVEY RESULTS

The questionnaire on bond issuing activities contained 16 questions. The first question was concerned with the *timing of bond issues* by enterprises. From the replies, it is clear that the number of enterprises that have issued bonds increased rapidly during the survey period. About three-quarters of the respondents indicated that their first issue of bonds was in 1987 or 1988 and about one-fifth of the respondents made more than one issuance in the past four years.

In order to examine the motivation and urgency of enterprises issuing bonds, the participants were asked whether they had other financing alternatives when the bonds were issued; about two-thirds of the respondents replied "yes," indicating that many of the enterprises indeed had a certain degree of financing options to exercise, including government investment fund allocation, bank loans, and issuing stocks. However, while most state-owned enterprises were still partially provided with government investment allocations or bank loans for their operations, collectively owned enterprises depended mainly on their own ability to raise capital.

When asked why they chose to issue bonds when they had other financing alternatives, almost half of the respondents said that they wanted to try this new form of financing even though they understood that the bond issuing process might be complicated and the financing cost high. Over one-third of the respondents indicated that they issued bonds because the funds raised through other channels were inadequate. Only a few respondents believed that the cost of issuing bonds was lower than that of other alternatives. The survey results also indicated that securing the supply of funds seemed to be more important to bond issuers than the cost of the capital, reflecting the overall situation in China and the general scarcity of investment funds.

For most of the state-owned enterprises, the cost of raising funds through bonds issuance was much higher than that of state-allocated investment funds and bank loans. During the period covered by the survey, the state banks charged an annual interest rate of only 7.2 percent for working capital loans and 10.4 percent for fixed-asset investment loans, while the interest rate paid on some bonds was as high as 15 percent per year. The dilemma in recent years, however, concerned the substantial difference between the funds needed by state-owned enterprises and the funds the state banks were able to provide. Therefore, a large number of state-owned enterprises, particularly those in sectors considered a low priority in the overall national economic development, had experienced a shortage of funds. To raise additional capital needed, they had to pay extra costs. For collectively owned enterprises, the funding of their operations through the banking system was virtually impossible.

How much debt did enterprises borrow through bond issuance to finance their operations? The survey revealed that, for over 80 percent of the enterprises, the funds raised through bond issuance accounted for less than 10 percent of their total financing. For some firms, it was even lower—below 5 percent. No enterprise obtained financing through bond issuance that exceeded 20 percent of the total financing needs, even though the state regulations stipulated that the total amount of debt financing through the bond issuance could be up to but not exceeding total assets (Figure 6.1). There was no indication that the percentage of debt financing through bond issuance was higher for collectively owned enterprises than for state-owned ones.

According to the survey, most of the bonds issued by enterprises so far had face values of either 50 yuan or 100 yuan, although some large denominations, such as 500, 1,000, and even 10,000 yuan were available to institutional investors. Bond maturities were relatively short. Only a fraction of the bonds issued had a maturity greater than three years (Figure 6.2). Maturities tended to be short since secondary markets for corporate bonds were not yet well established, and, therefore, longer-term bonds might not appeal to

Figure 6.1
Funds Raised Through Bonds (in percent of respondents)

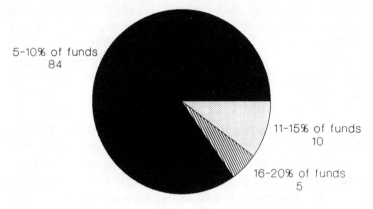

5-10% of funds
84

11-15% of funds
10

16-20% of funds
5

Source: Survey by the Authors.

bond investors. With the development of the secondary markets, however, it would be possible for enterprises to lengthen the maturity of the bonds to better fit their financing needs.

Interest rates offered to bondholders varied widely among issuers, ranging from 6 percent to 15 percent with the mean being about 10 percent (Figure 6.3). This range covered bonds with a maturity of one year to up to five years. Since March 1987, the regulation issued by the government has placed a cap on the interest rates that issuing enterprises could offer to investors. The highest interest rate a bond issuer could pay would be equal to the rate banks offer on time deposits of the same maturity plus a 40 percent risk premium. If a bank offered 10 percent on a one-year time deposit, the bond issuer could pay a 14 percent interest rate (the highest allowed to the bondholder) but could not exceed this level. The reason for the cap on interest rates was that the government believed that during the transitional period of the economy, when

Figure 6.2
Maturities of Bonds (in percent of respondents)

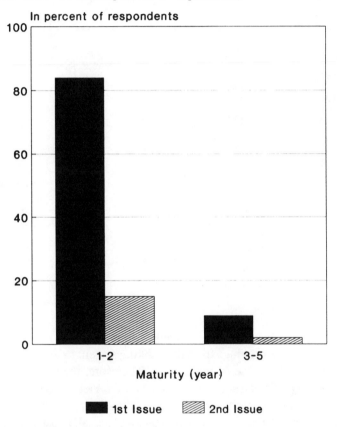

Source: Survey by the Authors.

planning and the market forces were both utilized to direct the economy, the market alone could not send correct signals.

Due to price distortions, enterprises that could offer higher interest rates might not necessarily have investment projects that were financially feasible or economically needed by the government. The authorities were afraid that if the limited funds were all invested in the sectors that did not produce real goods, it might not

Figure 6.3
Interest Rates of Bonds

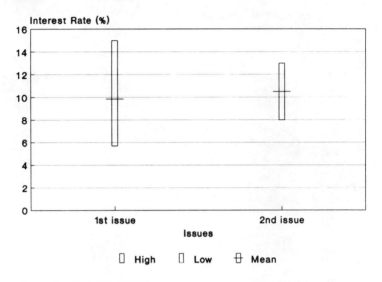

Source: Survey by the Authors.

benefit the economy as a whole, particularly if the investors withdrew their savings from the banking system to seek the higher returns of this type of investment. Therefore, they considered it necessary to place some restrictions on the yield of bonds, which would prevent enterprises from exceeding their capacities of debt servicing and thus avoid unnecessary and socially costly financial difficulties.

Prior to 1988, the interest rates paid on bonds issued by enterprises were different for individuals and institutional investors; rates were usually 2 to 3 percent lower for the institutional investors for the same bonds. This was due to the dual interest policies of the state banks, which had different deposit rates for institutional and household depositors. The primary purpose of this policy was to enable state banks to exercise control over identifiable segments of the depositors and to encourage enterprises to invest their surplus funds in productive facilities. If they had a temporary surplus to deposit with a bank or to invest, the return provided was not attractive. This created a big problem in the secondary market, in which enterprises could only transfer their securities to other enterprises. This dual-rate system was abandoned in 1988.

At the early stages of the bond-issuance activities, some bond issuers instituted other means to attract investors. For example, bondholders were eligible for lucky draws after each issuance was completed. The issuers would usually pay part of the coupons in cash and part in the form of a title to a lottery offering prizes ranging from an apartment or furniture to cash. The cost of funds to an issuer would be roughly equivalent to that of other issuers. The prizes were normally drawn within ten days of the completed sale of the issue. Those who did not win a prize would still earn the same interest rate, 2.4 percent per year as a savings account. This practice was gradually phased out in the primary bond market in order to standardize issuing activities.

The investors were also offered "bonds-in-kind" incentive schemes. When the bonds mature, the purchasers (most of them institutions) would have the option of being repaid both principal and interest in cash or in goods in kind such as cement, steel, supply of electricity, etc. These projects were usually involved in producing goods that were short in supply and, therefore, they could attract investors who needed the supply as well as the production inputs. In the survey, however, no respondents indicated that they had used this kind of arrangement in their bond issuing activities.

According to the survey results, 93 percent of the bonds were sold at face value. Only a few respondents indicated that the bonds were sold at a discount. In some cases, bonds were sold at face value to institutional investors but at a discount to individual investors. However, no reasons were given for these different treatments.

About two-thirds of the issuing enterprises indicated that they entrusted the local branch of the Central Bank or a trust and investment company to sell their bonds, since there were no specialized investment companies to do the underwriting. If the issuers were to sell 100 percent of bonds to their own employees, they usually handled the transactions and transfers by themselves. When they entrusted the bank to sell their bonds, it was because they needed outsider subscribers, even though the bonds were to be sold partly to their employees.

Among those enterprises that issued bonds to the public, there was no pattern in how much they sold to their own employees and how much they sold to the public. Generally, most of the enterprises sold bonds to their own employees for the first issue. After becoming more experienced with the issuing procedures, more and more enterprises tried public issuance to increase the amount of funds that could be raised (Figure 6.4). In the survey, about half of the respondents used public issuance. With regard to the use of the funds raised through bond issues, about one-third of the respondents indicated that they used the funds obtained to expand existing production capacity and a similar number of respondents said that they used the proceeds to make up working capital shortages. The rest indicated a variety of uses of their funds, including technical renovations, starting a new business, improving housing conditions for their employees, and building a commercial complex or other facilities that would be revenue producing (Figure 6.5).

The government paid increasing attention to the use of the funds raised from bond issuances. The increasing number of new projects financed by issuing securities has significantly aggravated the existing shortage or has created a new shortage in the supply of raw materials, energy, and transportation capacity. Consequently, the government decided to scrutinize the applications for approval of securities issues. In this process, issuers who attempted to use the financing to expand existing production facilities tended to get approval more easily than those who tried to raise capital for new projects.

Bonds that were sold to employees of the issuing enterprise were not allowed to be listed for trading in the secondary market. Therefore, most of the respondents (87 percent), including some of those that used public issuance, said that their bonds were not traded. With the secondary market for corporate bonds still under-

Figure 6.4
Types of Bond Buyers (in percent)

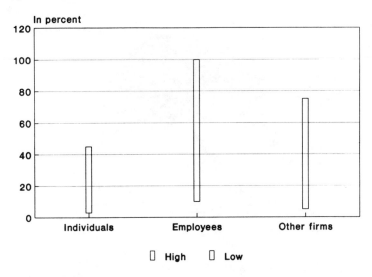

Source: Survey by the Authors.

developed, only a small fraction of bonds issued were traded (the operation of the secondary market will be discussed in detail in Chapter 8).

When comparing issuing bonds to obtaining bank loans, over one-third of the survey respondents indicated that issuing bonds was easier and more beneficial than borrowing funds from banks. About two-thirds of the respondents thought that issuing bonds was more complicated and less beneficial to the enterprises than obtaining bank loans. For most of the state-owned enterprises, obtaining funds by issuing bonds was not an easy job, considering the preparation of paperwork and the process involved to obtain approval. However, for most of the collectives that had no other financing alternatives, bond issuance was the only way to raise the badly needed funds.

Figure 6.5
Uses of Funds Raised Through Bond Issues (in percent of respondents)

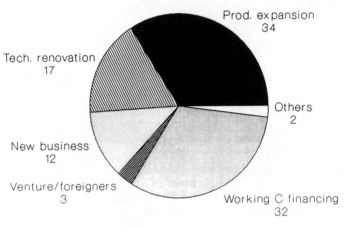

Prod. expansion
34

Tech. renovation
17

Others
2

New business
12

Venture/foreigners
3

Working C financing
32

Source: Survey by the Authors.

When asked whether they encountered restrictions on the disposal of the bond proceeds and on the amount of funds raised through issuing bonds, most respondents acknowledged the restrictions discussed above and indicated certain ways to avoid these restrictions. Basically, they tried to propose small projects for bond financing that would be relatively assured of approval by the financial authorities.

When asked whether they would like to issue bonds again based on their past experience, well over two-thirds (73 percent) of the respondents, including most of the collective-owned enterprise issuers, said "yes," since issuing bonds could help them raise needed capital. The rest, which consisted of many state-owned enterprises, were less willing to issue bonds again due to the higher financing cost and the work involved. The government policy stipulating that the amount of funds raised through issuing bonds would not be made available through the banking system, a policy intended to curtail the scale of investment activities, also affected the state-owned enterprises' motivation to issue bonds.

SUMMARY OF FINDINGS

1. The total amount of funds raised by the enterprises through issuing bonds far exceeded that of stocks, but was still insignificant when compared to other sources of financing, such as bank loans and government investment allocation. Most of the enterprises issuing bonds were state-owned, and were usually engaged in operations of substantial scale. Government regulations prohibited other types of enterprises from issuing bonds without special approval.

2. The yield on bonds issued by an enterprise was about 40 percent higher than the interest rate on time deposits of the same maturity. For the issuers, the cost of capital was about 20 percent higher than bank loans. The differences in bond yields for financing projects of different risk levels were almost negligible, due to the lack of a credit rating system. Some bonds contained payment-in-kind or lottery elements.

3. The maturities of bonds were mostly one to two years. The use of funds was under strict supervision of the local financial authority. Enterprises could not invest the bond proceeds in capital equipment without government approval. Lack of liquidity in the underdeveloped secondary market also prevented the issuer from issuing longer-term bonds.

4. A significant proportion of issuers sold bonds to their own employees. Public issuance was limited due to the lack of experience of the issuers.

5. Strong governmental control resulted in substantial restraints on market development. This was due to the government's fear of losing the control over the speed and scale of the market development and its implications for the economy as a whole. The immaturity of enterprises' behavior also indicated the need for strong governmental control. However, some of the state regulations had a negative impact on market development.

6. A large number of state enterprises felt that they lacked incentives to raise funds through bond issuance, considering the time-consuming procedures they had to go through to get approval and the higher costs they had to pay. Most collectives felt differently because they did not have all the sources of funds that were available to state-owned enterprises.

7

Stock Issuing Activities

The experiment with stock issues in China is still limited. Compared with bond issues, the number of enterprises issuing stocks and the amount of funds raised through stocks is rather small. The major bottleneck to the development of the stock market in China is inherent in China's economic system—mainly the state ownership. Technically, there are not enough private companies in China to foster a stock market.

THE OWNERSHIP ISSUE

As discussed in the previous chapter, state-owned enterprises have not been allowed to issue stocks by the Chinese government. The issue of ownership has been the main consideration. If state-owned enterprises were allowed to issue stocks to raise funds, it would raise a series of difficult questions: What would be the ownership identity of these enterprises?; How would the state handle the relationship with this type of enterprise?; and, To what extent should the state ownership be transformed? These are difficult economic and political issues.

The ownership issue has been debated not only in terms of the financing aspects of the enterprise, but more importantly in the context of broad economic reforms. The debate over this issue has been going on for a long time, focusing on the management aspects of the enterprises; that is, whether state ownership should be reformed in order to motivate proper economic behavior of the enterprise. If so, how would the state ownership be transformed?

In the 30-year period between 1949 and 1978, the Chinese government invested about 600 billion yuan in fixed assets in state-owned enterprises. If these state-owned enterprises were to be converted into private-owned ones, it would be impossible for the enterprises and individual investors to absorb this huge amount of assets. Many proposed that setting up joint-stock companies would be the best way to convert the state ownership system into a share system. The joint-stock companies would then combine the interests of the government, enterprises, employees, and other individual investors. Technically, the fixed assets invested by the government in an enterprise would be priced and converted into shares and owned by the government. The accumulated retained earnings of the enterprise, although difficult to calculate, would be converted into shares owned by the enterprise itself. The enterprise could also issue shares to its own employees or to other enterprises and individual investors. The board of directors, consisting of the representatives of all interested parties, would decide the management issues of the enterprise. The state would not withdraw its shares from the enterprise but would be able to transfer or sell them to other state entities.

However, transforming these proposal into reality would require time and effort. Before the ownership issue is fundamentally resolved, substantial involvement of state-owned enterprises in stock issuing activities is unlikely. So far, only a handful of state-owned enterprises have issued stocks as an experiment. The majority of enterprises that have issued stocks are collectively owned and joint-stock enterprises. Some new companies have also been set up with 100 percent of the initial capital being committed by the shareholders.

SURVEY RESULTS

The survey indicated that the shares outstanding for issuing companies ranged from less than one thousand to about two million. The majority of respondents in the survey indicated that their issues ranged from one thousand to ten thousand shares, while about one-quarter of the respondents issued more than ten thousand shares. The amount of funds raised was substantial for most of the issuing enterprises, particularly considering that most of them were engaged in small-scale business operations. More than two-thirds of the responding enterprises indicated that equity financing accounted for over 20 percent of their total assets.

The survey also revealed that the primary purpose of issuing stocks by these enterprises was to satisfy their financing needs rather than to change the ownership structure or the management of the enterprise. Only a few respondents replied that they issued stocks with the intention to affect the ownership structure (Figure 7.1). About two-thirds of the respondents noted that they issued stocks because they did not have other financing alternatives. For those with other sources of financing, the survey showed that they made the decision to issue stocks because they wanted to experiment with this new way of raising funds, and thought it would be beneficial to the management of their enterprise. They believed that once their employees had a personal interest in the enterprise through the purchase of the shares, it would be easier to motivate them to work more productively. Only a number of issuing enterprises replied that the funds raised through other sources were not adequate, and therefore they had to issue stocks to meet their additional needs.

As with bonds, most stock issuing enterprises sold stocks to their own employees. The primary reason was that these companies had no experience with stock issuances and therefore wanted to experiment with their own employees first. In this way, it would be easier to manage the issuance. Companies also wanted their employees to participate in the management of the enterprise in order to raise productivity, and in return, to benefit from the good performance of the enterprise (Figure 7.2).

According to the survey, the number of enterprises issuing stocks to the public was quite limited. These enterprises varied a great deal in size of operations, business lines, and operating

Figure 7.1
Purposes of Issuing Stocks (number of respondents)

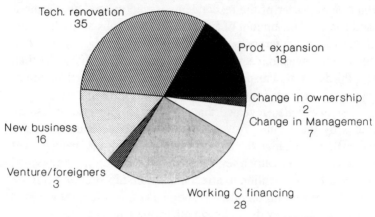

Tech. renovation
35

Prod. expansion
18

Change in ownership
2

Change in Management
7

New business
16

Venture/foreigners
3

Working C financing
28

Source: Survey by the Authors.

history. However, most of them sold a major proportion of their shares issued to outside investors, both individuals and institutions. When asked why they decided to sell stocks to the public, they listed a number of reasons. The major reasons were that they were confident that they could manage the issuance and that the amount of funds they wanted to raise was substantial.

The way the issuing enterprises distributed dividends to their shareholders was quite different from the Western method. At the very beginning, many enterprises offered investors a fixed amount of interest in the form of dividends. This method appeared to be logical at that time since most investors were not used to the concept of risk and had difficulty relating risk to investment return. If investors were told to buy stocks to share the profits and risks of a business, few people would be willing to do so. Many thought they could not afford to do this since their savings were very limited. Later on, as the issuing enterprises became more experienced and investors more accustomed to the risk–profit-sharing concept, the fixed amount of interest was gradually changed into

Figure 7.2
Types of Stock Buyers

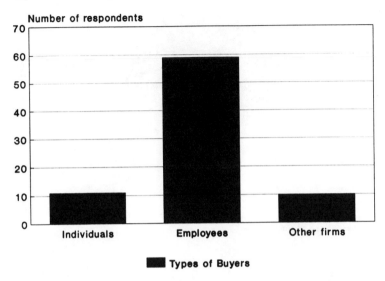

Source: Survey by the Authors.

a variable combination of a fixed amount of interest and dividends. The survey showed that this method of distributing earnings was used by most of the enterprises (Figure 7.3).

Over 90 percent of respondents distributed dividends annually. The rate of return for most stocks was between 11 and 15 percent. In some cases, it exceeded 20 percent (Figure 7.4). Based on this prevalent return level, and the fact that many enterprises had to keep a high dividend payment level in order to retain investors committed to their investment, the government later set an upper limit of 15 percent as the highest dividend an enterprise could pay to equity investors. When most of the enterprises could not fully control the major aspects of their operations, such as price and market, their behavior could not be expected to be very rational. Therefore, it was deemed necessary by the government to activate

Figure 7.3
Determination of Dividend Payments (in percent of respondents)

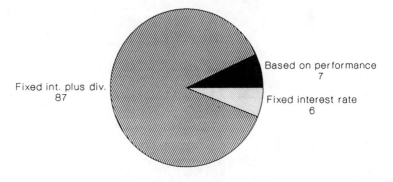

Based on performance
7

Fixed int. plus div.
87

Fixed interest rate
6

Source: Survey by the Authors.

Figure 7.4
Returns on Stocks (in percent of respondents)

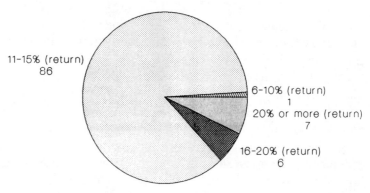

11-15% (return)
86

6-10% (return)
1

20% or more (return)
7

16-20% (return)
6

Source: Survey by the Authors.

restrictions in order to prevent unwanted competition on higher dividend payments to attract additional funds.

The risks involved in buying stocks were not fully understood by most investors. Many regarded buying shares as another type of personal savings account with a commercial bank, but realized they could get higher interest rates by investing in stocks than by putting money in the bank. In normal circumstances, the 15 percent dividend consisted of a 7.2 percent interest payment, which was basically guaranteed, and 7.8 percent of the dividend, which would vary according to the performance of the enterprise. However, most issuing enterprises tried to pay the highest dividends in order to keep their investors. Dividend payments were subject to a 20 percent tax, trimming the maximum real return on stock to 12 percent for investors.

Over half of the respondents held their board meetings regularly at intervals of one year, half-yearly, and quarterly, respectively. The remaining respondents held their board meetings only when needed. At these meetings, shareholder representatives would approve company charters, elect members to the board, and discuss issues concerning operations and management.

Most of the respondents (85 percent) regarded the issuing of stocks to finance the enterprise's operation as complicated but beneficial to the company. Over half said that they would like to issue more shares if the business needed extra financing, while many others declined to reply. When asked whether they felt pressure to improve the management and profitability of their enterprise in order to obtain better terms when they needed to issue bonds or stocks again, about half of the respondents said that they felt the pressure strongly, but the rest felt otherwise.

SUMMARY OF FINDINGS

1. Most of the enterprises issuing stocks were collectives. Funds raised through issuing stocks accounted for about 20 percent of all sources of capital for the collectives. Some newly established enterprises accumulated 100 percent of their capital by issuing

stocks. State-owned enterprises, with a few exceptions, were now prohibited from issuing stocks since the ownership issue was still a sensitive one and remained to be resolved, even though economic reform had resulted in substantial changes in China's economic structure.

2. Shares did not really represent the equity of an enterprise and thus did not necessarily represent ownership. The assets of the enterprise were not well-calculated before the stocks were issued. Therefore, the face value of the stock did not represent the true value of the enterprise's equity. The majority of stocks so far issued had a face value of 50 or 100 yuan.

3. The majority of issuing enterprises sold stocks to their own employees. Most enterprises wanted to experiment with their own employees first before trying to issue to the public. If the funds resulted in a good economic and financial rate of return, their employees could directly benefit from the enterprise and therefore were motivated to be more productive.

4. The majority of stocks issued guaranteed a certain percentage of return plus a variable dividend. The main reason for this was that individual investors did not have a good understanding of the risk and return involved in equity investment, including the issuers themselves. The issuers offered this kind of arrangement to attract investors and to make sure that their employees, if they were shareholders, could benefit from the performance of the enterprise. Many regarded buying stocks as another kind of savings account on which they could earn higher interest rates than in a bank.

5. The use of funds raised through issuing stocks was subject to government control. A substantial amount of funds raised through issuing stocks were not invested in capital equipment or in other inputs of production, but were used to satisfy short-term financial needs such as working capital requirements.

6. The issuing procedures were gradually being standardized with the implementation of more uniform regulations. The development of supporting institutions such as accounting, auditing, and securities companies had also exerted a positive influence on the process of formalizing stock issuing activities in China.

The findings of the survey illustrate the unique characteristics of China's emerging securities market and reflect the nature of the present economic system. Although some of the market practices were unique, or even incomprehensible to the outside world, they were not entirely unreasonable. To a great extent, these practices were indispensable as China's economy moved from central planning to a mixture of planning and market systems.

It could be said that the securities market in China was born prematurely and its development has been a difficult one. The economic reform, which actually triggered the emergence of the securities market, had given new life to the country's economy but had not yet provided a sufficiently favorable environment for the rapid growth of the securities market. In spite of the need for a more conducive environment, the market struggled to grow to a respectable size. Market capitalization reached about 20 billion yuan by 1991 (excluding government bonds, financial bonds, and bonds for financing key infrastructural projects) and the importance of the market had begun to be recognized. In the process, an increasing number of individuals and institutions have learned about the market itself and how to participate, utilize, and regulate it, all of which will be crucial to its future development.

8

Securities Trading Activities and Exchanges

With the proliferation of securities issuing activities by enterprises, it became evident that a secondary market for these securities should be established to support further development of the primary market. On August 5, 1986, the first bond trading center was set up in Shenyang. One month later, bonds and stocks began to be traded in Shanghai. The international financial community was very much impressed by these events and referred to these two initial trading centers as "stock exchanges," titles these institutions were hesitant to assume. Despite their small size and primitive mode of operation, the opening of this kind of trading center represented another important milestone in China's financial development history.

Following the Shenyang and Shanghai model, trading centers quickly appeared in other major cities such as Xian, Tianjin, Chongqin, Harbin, and Ningpo. The number of trading centers in each of these cities increased from one to several. For example, by the end of 1988 the number of trading centers in Shanghai had reached six. Later in 1990, these centers merged. This chapter summarizes the results of the survey, including the interviews and the responses to the questionnaire, regarding the secondary market activities in China.

THE OPERATION OF SECONDARY SECURITIES MARKETS

Trading Centers and Regulatory Framework

Prior to 1990, the secondary market of securities in China consisted of trading centers. These centers could hardly be called stock exchanges due to their physical set-up and their limited scale of operation. Except for those in Shanghai, most of them were fairly small and were not equipped with modern communication equipment or facilities for handling large-volume trading. Most transactions in these trading centers were processed with the help of only an abacus or calculator and were recorded in longhand. The trading activities at each center were not connected via a network. The more active trading centers usually had no more than a few dozen staff members, including traders, brokers, administrative, and logistic staff. In most cases, trading centers were run by the local branch of the Central Bank or by a trust and investment unit of a bank. The same organization also often sold new issues. In a sense, therefore, the primary and secondary markets were the same one.

There was no formal legislation governing the operation of secondary markets nor an independent agency to enforce the law. However, some rules (such as the following) were established by the Central Bank to govern trading. Local branches of the Central Bank also worked out detailed rules for local trading centers to follow. These basic rules were that:

1. trading centers could only handle securities that had been approved by the Central Bank;
2. transactions must be conducted on a cash basis. No futures were allowed to be traded;
3. trading centers must make delivery and settlement within a specified time period. The clearance would be done inside the trading facilities;
4. prices for the listed securities should not fall below the face value of those particular securities and the trading center was prohibited from trading securities at a price much higher than the face value;

5. the income of the exchange should be derived mainly from trading, which would be the difference between the selling and buying prices and the commissions;

6. a trading center could determine the number of brokers working for it and could provide temporary credit to them if needed. The trading center would also serve as a last resort if anything happened to the brokers;

7. a trading center was required to pay the reserve requirement to the Central Bank, but at a lower rate than other financial institutions; and

8. the trading center was required periodically to report trading activities to the Central Bank and report them on a timely basis if a major fluctuation occurred.[1]

These rules, although far from comprehensive, were determined based on prevailing conditions under which trading activities would take place. They were temporary guidelines for the trading centers to follow in their operations.

Trading Services

The type of securities that were handled by these trading centers included the following: financial bonds, bonds issues for special investment projects, corporate bonds, and stocks. Because the total volume of securities issued was small and consisted of mostly new issues, there seemed to be no need to have separate market places for trading different securities. Therefore, they were all traded in one place and were handled by the same group of brokers. Bonds and stocks issued by enterprises to the public could be traded in trading centers. Treasury bonds were also traded in many centers. In terms of volume, treasury bonds accounted for over half of the securities that have been issued.

Listing Requirements

Only a very small number of bonds and stocks issued were listed for trading on these trading centers. Shenyang, for example, only listed bonds issued by over 20 enterprises among the more than two thousand enterprises that had issued bonds or stocks at the time when the survey took place. The same was true in Shanghai, which had listed only eight stocks and two bonds. There were a few reasons why the trading in the secondary market was so light: First, as discussed in Chapters 6 and 7, the majority of bonds and stocks thus far issued were mainly sold to employees of the issuing enterprises. Some of the enterprises did not even issue certificates but made an entry on the books of the enterprise. Therefore, they were not allowed to be listed with trading centers.

Second, securities trading was new to most Chinese. Even those who had experience when Shanghai had a stock exchange 40 years ago were not sure what to do about the new trading center. As far as the listing requirement was concerned, they did not have specific rules. They chose a number of companies that issued bonds or stocks to the public and thoroughly examined their prospectus and other records. If the trading center believed that the companies were strong, well-managed, and would be good for their business, they would list them for trading.

Third, securities trading was also constrained by the centers' inability to handle large volumes. Within only a few years after the securities market started, newly issued securities reached about 10 billion yuan. How to allow this amount of securities to be properly transferred among investors was no easy task for the new market. Above all, due to the unique economic and social environments in China, it was almost impossible to copy another country's model. Consequently, trading centers had to work out their own trading procedures step by step and make improvements gradually along with the overall development of the market.

Trading Procedures

Most of the trading centers opened for trading every day, including Sundays. But some opened only a few days per week, depending on the expected trading volume. Trading procedures and fee levels varied to some extent in each city but they generally followed similar procedures. At the listed buying and selling prices, the trading center bought stocks or bonds from the holder who wished to sell and then resold them to the investors who wished to buy. The difference in the buying and selling prices was the profit of the trading center. The difference between the number of shares bought and sold became the inventory of the trading center.

The centers also allowed alternative ways of trading: (a) the buyer or seller could set a price and trust the trading center to find a matching buyer or seller, but the buyer needed to put down a 20 percent deposit for such an arrangement. If the deal was completed based on the quoted prices, the trading center would charge a commission; (b) the seller and buyer could freely negotiate a price inside the trading facility and have their transactions certified by the trading center to prevent fake certificates. The certified transfer would then become eligible for future transfers at the trading center. In return, the trading center would charge a fee, usually 0.5 percent of the face value of the certificate, from both the buyer and seller; (c) if the holder of the certificate needed cash but did not wish to sell, he could sign an agreement with the trading center to get cash and use the certificate as collateral. The individual would then have ten days to three months to repurchase the certificates; however, beyond that time period, the certificate would automatically belong to the trading center. The trading center would also charge a fee for this type of transaction, usually 0.3 percent of the face value. These alternative methods, however, accounted for only a small portion of the total trading activities.

Pricing Mechanism

The pricing mechanism on these trading centers was quite different from that in the stock exchanges of Western countries. The auction system was not used for continuous price setting for all the bonds and stocks listed. The selling and buying prices listed on these trading centers were artificially set based on the following factors: (a) interest rates; (b) the loss and gain of the sellers and buyers; and (c) the supply and demand for that particular type of security. In the case of bonds, the interest rate of the bond and the maturity were taken into consideration.

The following provides an example on how prices are determined on China's "stock exchanges." Suppose a particular bond with a 100-yuan face value has an annual interest rate of 12 percent. If the holder of that bond decided to sell the bond (bonds less than three months old are not allowed to be traded), the trading center would price that bond in the following manner: it would lower the interest rate for that bond from the current 1 percent to 0.66 percent per month (with reference to the bank deposit rate). Therefore, a 100-yuan bond of over three, six, or nine months old would be priced at 102 yuan (100 + 100 x 0.66 percent × 9). Bonds of over one year old would be sold at the original interest rate. Besides the discount of the interest rate, bondholders also had to pay 1 percent of the face value as a commission to the trading center, thus bringing the actual yield of a three-month-old bond to about 4 percent, a little higher than a demand deposit, and bringing the yield of six-month bond to 6 percent, a little higher than a three-month time deposit. The same formula would apply to longer maturities.

The purpose of this kind of pricing mechanism, according to authorities, was to prevent investors from selling their certificates without careful consideration, as well as consideration for the trading centers' lack of facilities and capabilities to handle large volumes of trading. In addition, this kind of pricing mechanism could help to avoid speculation while maintaining the liquidity and stability of the markets. Trading centers' officials believed that this kind of pricing mechanism was feasible and viable given China's current market conditions.

The pricing of stock, which was mostly affected by the performance of the company and the availability of shares for trading were less restricted than bonds. For example, take the stock of Yanzhong Industrial Company and Feile Acoustic Company (based in Shanghai). Their shares started to be traded at Shanghai Jing An Trading Center in September 1986 at an initial price of 50 yuan per share. By the end of 1987, Yanzhong shares were traded at about 55 yuan per share, and Feile at about 57 yuan. The center officials believed that the following two factors contributed to the higher price of Feile stock: (a) the company's board decided that the company would pay a 20 percent dividend tax for its shareholders; (b) the quality of Feile products was good and its management was strong. Moreover, Feile had issued only five hundred thousand yuan of shares compared with Yanzhong's five million yuan of shares. The fact that many individuals chased after a few good investment choices also pushed up the stock price.

With the current pricing mechanism, the price for a particular bond or stock could remain unchanged for many days. For example, in the 80 days from March 27 to June 27, 1987, prices on the Shenyang trading center changed on average only four times, with a few of them changing seven or eight times, according to trading center officials.

Bonds and stocks of a company could be listed on several trading centers to facilitate the buying from and the selling to the public. For the time being, if one wanted to buy or sell bonds or stocks, one had to come to the trading center. No transactions were conducted by telephone. Each trading center decided the price for a particular type of securities. Due to the lack of communication facilities, sometimes the same stock had different prices at different trading centers.

Trading Activities

Many observers had an impression that trading activities on these trading centers were slow, particularly considering the pricing mechanism they had been using. In fact, however, the trading activities on these centers were quite impressive as illustrated by the following statistics.

From March 1987 to December 1987, the Shenyang trading center bought 5.6 million yuan worth of certificates and sold 4.19 million yuan, which was 17,000 yuan per working day on average.[2] From January to June 1988, Shanghai Jing An trading center concluded transactions worth 53.82 million yuan,[3] which was an increase of 13 times over the same period of the previous year. At the very beginning, the trading was slow but it picked up a great deal of momentum during 1988. Driven by a sharp increase of household savings and declining bank interest rates, the turnover on the Shanghai exchange reached 4 billion yuan in 1990 and the 1991 trading volume from two exchanges, Shanghai and Shenzhen, is expected to double that in 1990.[4]

Among the four main types of securities that are traded on trading centers, the most actively traded, comparatively speaking, were corporate bonds. Others were less active owing to the following reasons:

1. The total volume of stocks issued was small. Holders of stocks, particularly those being paid good dividends, were unwilling to sell them. The buying and selling ratio for the Yanzhong Industrial Company and Feile Acoustics Company, for example, was 11:1 during the survey period, according to the officials on the Shanghai Jing An trading center; and

2. Financial bonds issued so far carried very attractive terms, with interest rates far exceeding that on deposits for the same maturity; therefore buyers far exceed sellers. Bonds for special investment projects had similar features and were relatively new issues.

Among corporate bonds, those that had lottery arrangements were the most actively traded. Once the drawing results were known, those who did not win a prize were willing to sell the bond and invest in other securities. For regular bonds that carried good interest payments, holders were less willing to sell them unless they needed cash for an emergency.

In short, the following factors were believed to have contributed to the low trading volume: (a) the securities issued were very attractive, and therefore holders had little incentive to sell; (b) the price movement was small due to the pricing mechanism used; and (c) holders of securities did not have to worry about the risks involved in the investment.

MAJOR PROBLEMS

When officials at the trading centers were asked what they thought the major problems of securities trading activities were, they agreed that the pricing mechanism, the limited number of listed securities, and lack of modern communication facilities and experienced professional staff were of great concern. However, they also noted that further development of the primary market, where more standardized and quality securities were issued, and more infrastructural development for the whole securities industry were also important to the improvement and perfection of the secondary market. The general public's knowledge of the investment and financial markets and of ideological change would also be important for dynamic operation of the trading center.

SUMMARY OF MAJOR FINDINGS

Although the secondary market for the securities issued in China emerged only a few years ago, it has made substantial progress in terms of operational procedures and volume traded. The market has the following characteristics:

1. Trading practices, particularly the pricing mechanisms, are substantially different from those of other countries. Prices are artificially set to eliminate the possibility of manipulative and speculative buying and selling. The current procedures work toward maintaining a stable market but not necessarily an efficient market, where demand and supply are truly reflected.

2. The trading volume, although substantially increased from its very slow beginning, is still very low compared to emerging markets in other countries. The trading volume is restrained by the limited number of listed securities for trading and the lack of an adjusting mechanism in the market due to inflexible pricing, which often results in an imbalance between buying and selling with demand far exceeding supply.

3. Price movement is slight and only occasional. Holders of securities have little incentive to sell. Investment information is sketchy and not readily available.

4. Although trading procedures in China are different from those of other countries, they prove to be practical and necessary to the current developmental stage of the securities market in China. They serve one of the basic purposes of a secondary market, providing liquidity to investors.

5. The emergence of the secondary market has exerted a positive impact on the primary market. New issues are more formalized and standardized in order to qualify for trading on the secondary market, and to attract more investors.

6. Lack of modern facilities and experienced professional staff handicap the trading centers which are unable to handle large volumes of trading.

7. Further development of the secondary market depends on the development of the primary market and the infrastructural improvement for the securities industry, such as the legal framework for trading and the availability of information to all who want to participate in the securities market. The current operating procedures should not be replaced by the more standard procedures of other countries unless the above-mentioned improvements are achieved.

SHANGHAI SECURITIES EXCHANGE

Introduction

The Shanghai Securities Exchange (SSE) was formally re-established in November 1990, an outcome of the less well-organized "trading centers" that were discussed in the previous chapter. While the immediate objective of establishing the formal stock exchange is to help enterprises in the Shanghai area raise capital more efficiently, the ultimate goal of the SSE is more ambitious. Indeed, the Shanghai government, consistent with the central government's long-term plan, aims to reinstate Shanghai as an influential financial center in Asia. The establishment of the SSE is, therefore, the first step toward this end.[5]

Development of the Shanghai Securities Market

In 1986, the Shanghai branch of the People's Bank of China decided to develop the Shanghai securities market through two steps: first, to set up an over-the-counter (OTC) market; and second, based on the OTC market, to establish a securities exchange. By 1990 the OTC market had achieved a considerable degree of success and business had expanded rapidly. Also, significant work had been done to establish and improve the regulatory and institutional framework governing the development of the securities market.

Since the establishment of "trading centers" in 1984, and particularly since 1988, the trading volume of various types of securities in the secondary market has increased sharply. For example, total trading volume of all types of securities averaged roughly 40 million yuan between 1984 and 1987, while in 1988 it increased to 300 million yuan and in 1989 it rose further to approximately 1.0 billion yuan. In the first half of 1990, the trading volume reached 1.6 billion yuan. During the same period, trading volume in the Shanghai market accounted for about 50 percent of total trading nationwide and due to this rapidly developing market, substantial amount of capital flowed from other provinces to the Shanghai securities market.

In November 1991 the Central Bank approved ten new stock listings for Shanghai, increasing the total listings from eight to eighteen. The total capitalization of the market has also increased from approximately five to ten billion yuan. Along with the active trading in the secondary market, the number of enterprises that issued stock and bonds increased significantly, from a few hundred to about 3,000 enterprises by the end of 1990. Also, a credit rating corporation was established, providing credit rating services to securities issuers and investors.

With the development of the securities market, the desire for securities investment also grew steadily. By the end of 1990, almost 1 percent of the total population in Shanghai took part in securities trading activities. At the same time, institutional investors, including insurance corporations, retirement funds (pension funds), and social welfare institutions, also grew rapidly and have started to participate in security trading activities.

Characteristics of the SSE

The SSE claims to be a non-profit legal entity, presently consisting of 25 members (all institutions). The general membership meeting is the most powerful organization while the decision-making organization is the board of directors. There are three managing directors, a general manager, a president, and a vice president. The general manager is in charge of daily operations of the SSE and is the legal representative of the SSE.

The business scope of the SSE is as follows:

1. To provide for organized trading of securities;
2. To manage spot trading of listed securities;
3. To provide securities clearing and delivery services;
4. To provide securities transfer and organized storage services; and
5. To provide market information.

The securities listed in the SSE mainly include government, financial, and corporate bonds and stocks. The SSE allows enterprises from other parts of the country to list their securities on the exchange. At present, there are approximately 30 types of securities listed on the exchange including five government bonds, nine financial bonds, eight corporate bonds, and eight stocks.

Currently, only spot trading is allowed in the SSE. Transaction categories are divided into the trading of one day, regular day, and appointed day. The trading amount must be a set lot or its multiple. Brokers trade in securities according to the principle of time and price priority. The delivery and settlement of securities is carried out according to the net quota receivable and payable as balanced by the brokers and settled by the settlement department in the same period of settlement. The net quota of securities receivable and payable is collected and preserved after it has been balanced and registered in the securities storage account. The ownership of various stocks is transferred only by the settlement department.

The quotation on the market is displayed on the trading floor's screen and transmitted by electronic computer network to all the brokers' counters. Meanwhile, comprehensive and authorized quotations, analysis, and forecasts are supplied by newspapers, magazines, television, and radio stations.

On the trading floor, computers, broadcasting instruments, and monitors have been installed. There are two trading counters and forty-six trading seats with direct and indirect telephone lines and a computer terminal for each trader. Facsimiles, teletypewriters, and duplicators are available for use in the telecommunication center.

SHENZHEN STOCK EXCHANGE

The Shenzhen Stock Exchange was also formally established in 1990. Initially, five companies were listed in the Exchange, including the Shenzhen Development Bank, Anda Transport Stock Company Ltd., Wanke Enterprise Stock Company Ltd., Gintain Business Stock Company Ltd., and Yuanye Business Stock Company Ltd. In November 1991 the Central Bank approved another 11 companies to be listed on the exchange, thus raising the market capitalization from about 4.0 billion yuan to about 8.0 billion.

The evolution of the Shenzhen stock market started in 1986, when some companies were allowed to experiment with the Joint Stock System. In 1988, the Shenzhen Development Bank first began to sell stocks publicly in the market. As of the end of 1991, there were more than 200 companies in Shenzhen under the Joint Stock System.

Like other stock markets in the world, the Shenzhen stock market has also been heavily influenced by both political and economic factors. Following the "June 4 Incident" of 1989, the average price of the stocks listed dropped by over 30 percent. Soon after, however, stock prices rebounded sharply. In order to curb sharp price movements, rules were issued that price increases would not exceed 1 percent per day while price decreases would not exceed 5 percent. (These rules were later abolished.) During 1990, average stock prices rose more than 11 times, due to remarkable performances of issuing companies and the continued short supply of stocks in the market.[6]

Looking ahead, the Shenzhen Stock Exchange is planning to list the stocks of another ten companies in 1992 and to allow foreign companies to be listed on the Exchange, thus making Shenzhen one of the largest financial centers in China.

NOTES

1. These rules are summarized from the Interim Regulation on Securities Trading by Shanghai Branch of the People's Bank. No official translation is currently available.

2. *China Finance*, April 1988, 45.

3. *People's Daily*, Overseas Edition, August 16, 1988.

4. *Financial Times*, April 26, 1991.

5. A good discussion on stock exchanges in China in general and the Shanghai and Shenzhen Stock exchanges in particular can be found in "China Marches to a Changing Turn," *Euromoney*, August 1990, 46-50.

6. See "China Marches to a Changing Turn," *Euromoney*, August 1990, 46-50; Adi Ignatius, "For Chinese Speculators, the Streets Offer Better Deals Than the Stock Exchange," *Wall Street Journal*, July 6, 1990, 4; and Shuzhong Li and Guanghuai He, "A Look into Shenzhen's Stock Craze," *Intertrade*, April 1991, 26-27.

9

Prospects for Future Development

Pioneering, primitive, premature, and promising is how China's fledgling securities experimentation can be described. The issuing and trading of securities undoubtedly opens an important avenue for China's financial development. Securities provide a potentially important source of financial autonomy and flexibility, particularly for China's rapidly expanding collective and private sectors, as well as for state-owned enterprises. Although the securities market is still small in scale, it is expected to play an important role in China's economic reform and in its increasingly competitive and complex financial system.

The securities market is markedly underdeveloped in China in terms of the (a) amount of investment capital raised; (b) range of securities available; (c) volume of transactions in the secondary market; and (d) development of the necessary legal framework, financial intermediaries, regulatory bodies, and supporting institutions and facilities. However, the importance of securities in establishing a better financial market has begun to be recognized. It is also evident that the capital market cannot fully play its role of allocating resources without an efficient financial system.

The major findings contained in this book indicate that the current practices and procedures of new securities issues and of the transfer of existing ones are very different from those of other countries. Many practices and procedures adopted in the West and other advanced developing countries do not necessarily suit China's needs. The unique market practices and procedures used so far by the Chinese have proven to be indispensable as China's economy moves from a centrally planned one to a mixture of planning and market forces.

The current securities market in China is influenced heavily by government policies and regulations. Its structure and characteristics are not the outcome of a natural evolutionary process. Rather they reflect strong government intervention in deciding how the market should be developed and utilized to the best interest of the economy and the country. Government intervention is an impeding factor in the overall securities market development; however, some restrictions are warranted in view of the unfavorable environment for a too rapid and uncontrolled growth of the market.

Despite these constraints, the potential for market development exists. Estimates indicate that China will need a 400 billion yuan investment fund in this decade to quadruple its gross industrial and agricultural output by the end of this century, the goal set by the modernization program. If 350 million Chinese individuals, about a quarter of the total population, invest 100 yuan in securities each year for 12 years, the investment funds required would be raised, excluding institutional investors. Therefore, the role of the securities market is too important to be neglected. The key issue is how to improve the market environment, functions, and mechanisms to allow it to play a full role. If the market is allowed to develop further, China's market capitalization could easily equal that of Korea, Malaysia, or Thailand.

MARKET DEVELOPMENT PROSPECTS

The future of China's securities market, as an effective function of mobilizing long-term investment capital and promoting allocative efficiency, depends on the progress of the following aspects of China's economy: (a) the deepening of the economic reform and of the management reform of Chinese enterprises; (b) further maturation of China's financial sector; (c) further improvement in infrastructure for the securities industry; and (d) favorable government policies. The focus of this section is to analyze these fundamental factors that are restraining market development.

Deepening of the Economic Reform

The progress of the economic reforms in China, including financial reforms, has had a direct impact on the emergence of the securities market. Further development of the securities market will depend upon the success of these economic reforms. The current practices, which are far from the standardized operations widely used in other countries, are designed to cope with the current environment and accommodate the present economic system. Therefore, the future development and gradual formalization of the market must be supported by fundamental changes in the overall economic system.

Although great progress was made in restructuring China's economic system during the past 11 years, qualitative results have not yet been achieved. The reforming of these systems has proven to be extremely complex. In the investment system, interest-bearing loans have begun to replace fiscal appropriations of investment grants in most sectors, but budgetary allocation, while reduced, is still an important source of financing for state-owned enterprises. Government involvement in the allocation of funds for investment and in financial decisions must be further reduced to allow the market and financial intermediaries to play an adequate role, both in terms of the level and direction of investment. Only in this manner can enterprises have more autonomy in their financial decisions and management.

The ownership issue needs to be resolved before state-owned enterprises can fully utilize the equity market for raising risk capital. Transforming the state-owned enterprises has become imperative. According to official statistics released in August 1988, about 17 percent of the total of more than 6,000 key state-owned enterprises are losing money due to policy shortcomings and inefficient management. Establishing a wide-ranging shareholding system is expected to improve industrial performance. Only when state enterprises of good size and strength participate in the equity market will the market show great vitality. Capital market development will mean that the excessive emphasis on public sector enterprises must be significantly reduced, and that the economic and financial role of an efficient and dynamic private sector must be expanded.

Further Maturation of the Financial Sector

The current development stage of China's financial sector has been discussed in great detail in Chapter 4, with an emphasis on the relationship between the development of a securities market and the overall development of China's financial sector. Capital markets play an important role in industrialized countries and are beginning to do so in a number of developing nations. However, the development of a capital market must be consistent with the overall development of the financial sector of a country. Future developments of China's financial sector that will benefit its capital market includes: (a) a more market-oriented and integrated structure of interest rate and its determination; (b) continued reduction of government involvement in credit allocation; (c) growth of institutional investors such as insurance companies, pension funds, and investment trusts, which typically are the driving force behind many developed securities markets and; (d) dissemination of the knowledge of the benefits of financial savings, the functions and characteristics of different financial instruments, and specific investment techniques.

Development of Infrastructure for the Securities Industry

If the use of securities for raising long-term capital is expected to expand further in China, it will be necessary to permit and to expand the operations of securities brokers and brokerage firms specializing in underwriting and marketing new issues. Their operations should gradually be integrated into a simple electronic trading network with a series of trading floors, effectively bringing together total demand and supply.

Another critical aspect is the number and quality of securities industry professionals in terms of their technical skills and analytical ability. China could benefit from investing in training programs, which would combine government and industry efforts and involve foreign securities companies to disseminate professional knowledge and upgrade the professional quality of the securities industry as a whole.

A comprehensive legal framework is another important factor in the development of a capital market as its operational efficiency depends, to a great extent, upon laws and regulations pertaining to companies, banks, investment firms, securities exchange, commercial accounting, and taxation. At present, the laws and regulations that would provide the necessary framework for the development of a modern capital market have not been established. Moreover, the authority for regulating the issuance of bonds and stocks rests with the country's central bank. Due to potential conflicts of interest arising from the responsibility for both the banking system and the securities market, many countries have preferred to create a separate regulatory agency to oversee the issuance and trading of bonds and stocks and to enforce its regulations independent of political pressures and influences.

The enforcement and supervision of public disclosure requirements are also crucial to the prevention of fraudulent market behavior, such as misstating or hiding the current situation and prospects of a borrowing entity. Investors determine the underlying value of risk capital only if they are well-informed about the present financial situation of the enterprise in which they would invest and its prospects for future growth and financial stability. Such an informed judgment is only possible on the basis of the availability of the information provided by companies. Good information is needed not only for outside investors but also for professional managers and bank lenders. Therefore, accounting and auditing principles, as well as legislation on disclosure by companies whose risk capital is sold to outside investors, must be strictly enforced.

China has also considered establishing procedures and agencies for credit rating that would classify bonds issued by enterprises, municipalities, financial institutions, and other issuers into various risk categories. This would help institutional investors maintain a diversified and prudent portfolio, and would help individual investors determine how risky their investments are.

Favorable Policies of the Government

Government policies have had a significant influence on capital market development in many developing countries. Government policies are crucial to the establishment of an environment of investor confidence through the maintenance of political stability, steady economic growth with low inflation, and support for the private sector. In China's case, government policies on the level and structure of interest rates, the allocation of credit among sectors and between public and private enterprises, and the regulations governing the financial institutions and individual investors as well as the level of taxation, are essential for capital market development.

Tax policy is one of the most powerful instruments for stimulating capital market activity available to a government since it can affect the level of savings and investment and the relative demand for various types of financial assets. The current tax on dividend income (20 percent) disfavors securities investors, while interest earnings on bank deposits are not subject to any tax. Although tax incentives are critical for developing capital markets, it must be recognized that governments have other priorities that must be considered as well.

The evolution of China's emerging securities market into a sophisticated Western-style capital market will be a long process. Many problems commonly associated with securities markets take a completely different form in a planned economy, and therefore cannot simply be resolved by borrowing rules and concepts from the West. China needs to establish rules that suit its development needs. A securities market cannot be an isolated development. It is closely related to the level of economic development and to the financial sector. The changes in economic and financial systems in China could create the possibility of the existence of the market, but still await a truly favorable environment.

As promised during the October 1991 annual meeting of the International Monetary Fund and World Bank, China has continued its policies of economic reform and has allowed foreign investment in the Shanghai and Shenzhen stock markets on a limited scale.

Late last November there was a virtual stampede of applicants in the Shenzhen Special Economic Zone to buy shares in eleven Chinese companies. These "A" shares were sold in yuan and offered only to Chinese citizens. While this marked a significant change in China's financial structure, more changes were yet to come. On Christmas Day 1991, U.S. $10.9 million of "B" shares, redeemable in foreign currency and available only to foreigners, were floated on the Shenzhen market. Sixteen million of these China Southern Glass shares representing 14.9 percent of the glass-making venture were easily placed by Hoare Govett Asia Ltd. However, these shares of China Southern Glass were not the only offering of "B" shares. An offering of U.S. $74 million in "B" shares of the Shanghai Vacuum Electronic Device Company quickly followed on the Shanghai exchange. The offering of these "B" shares elicited an overwhelming response from foreign financial institutions and within just a few weeks, over 25 percent of Shanghai Vacuum's shares were purchased by foreign buyers. By dividing its public offerings into two classes, "A" shares for domestic investors only and "B" shares restricted to foreign investors only, China hopes to control the amount of investment capital flowing into its markets and curb speculation.

Investors, however, often refer to the speculative nature of investing in China with its lack of clear regulations concerning such basic issues as settlement and disclosure procedures. Yet

China's lack of corporate law, ambiguous trading mechanisms, and questionable accounting practices have done little to stem the rapid growth of its securities markets. While the securities market in Shanghai, which opened in December 1990, is six months older than the market in Shenzhen, Shenzhen's market capitalization is now triple that of Shanghai's market. According to analysts at the JF China Investment Company, Shenzhen's market will account for 96 percent of the estimated five billion yuan of shares in Chinese companies to be issued to foreigners.[1]

The opening of China's securities market to foreign investors marks a turning point in the emergence of China as an internationally competitive developing nation. The expansion of China's stock listings and the privatization of some of its state enterprises will help absorb China's extraordinarily high levels of domestic savings by both individuals and enterprises. Increased development of China's financial markets and its economic and regulatory reforms will facilitate China's ability to assess and meet true market driven supply and demand. As China's investment requirements outpace its traditional sources of funds, it must continue to make significant efforts to attract direct foreign investment and participate actively in international financial markets. These steps are critical if China is to raise the funds it needs for its modernization program.

As noted in the Asian *Wall Street Journal* in October 1991,[2] the People's Bank of China has now lost the limited independence it had gained over the previous decade. "Although banking officials continue to play lip service to economic efficiency, they have been taking their cue from the powerful state planning commission as they pump billions of dollars into inefficient state factories or unprofitable projects that are deemed important by planners." As a result of this indiscriminant lending, "loans are growing at a rapid pace. Loans outstanding at the end of June 1991 rose 22 percent from a year earlier. Cash in circulation has also been rising rapidly this year [1991]—up 20 percent at the end of June from a year earlier [1990]—and that poses an inflationary threat."

While these measures have indeed provided a much needed boost to the economy, they have also added to the inflationary impact. Industrial output rose by a little more than 13.5 percent in the first ten months of 1991, compared with negligible growth in 1990. Chinese officials projected a growth of 8 percent in GNP for 1991, with much of the growth coming from the South and East, particularly Guangdong Province, Shanghai, and special economic zones, including Shenzhen. Most foreign joint ventures, as well as highly productive collectives and many free-market entrepreneurs, are located in these areas. Government funds, however, had been channeled to the inefficient state factories that continue to build inventories of goods unwanted even in the Chinese market. The rationale is to maintain production and wages at any cost for political purposes; however, this effort does little to build the economy and, in fact, is most likely to prove a negating factor because it will reignite the inflationary impacts if it continues to be sustained.

Instead, a much wiser move would be to expand stock market listings, including privatization of some of the state enterprises, in order to absorb the extraordinarily high levels of domestic savings by both individuals and enterprises. China's domestic savings rate is currently at 40 percent of disposable income, with the pool of private savings estimated at 1 trillion yuan. Consequently, the demand for purchase of local securities in China is indeed great. For example, when the Shanghai Xinye real estate shareholding company placed a limited number of shares for sale to the public in August 1991, approximately 200,000 people lined up to buy shares.[3] Similar situations exist whenever any stock is made available.

For the foreseeable future, China's securities market is likely to be strictly for those investors whose only other alternative is a Chinese currency account. However, China has already examined the possible benefits and costs of allowing foreign portfolio investment, and has allowed foreign investors to participate in two stock flotations of "B" shares. The issuing of a separate class of shares for foreign investors is a common practice and is used in other developing countries, such as the Philippines and Thailand. However, the role of foreign institutional investors in China's stock markets is yet to be determined.

Another initial step might be for Sino-foreign joint ventures in China to issue bonds and shares in the Chinese currency for domestic investors, and in foreign currency for foreigners. Chinese partners have been unable to meet their financial commitments and local borrowing is not available to most Sino-Chinese joint venture firms. Furthermore, the foreign partners are unwilling to invest additional amounts; in most cases, because of the uncertainties that exist in China.

China lags far behind its Asian neighbors in opening its stock markets to foreign investors. For example, both Thailand and Indonesia provide virtually open access to their markets. The Thai Fund, similar to the Korean Fund, has been extremely successful in terms of raising capital. Such a move by China would not only enhance its external financial position, but would also be a significant factor in fostering growth and development of its industrial sector.

POSSIBLE FUTURE COURSES OF ACTION

The following recommendations for policy and strategy changes are provided for further development of the securities market in China.

Implementing a Comprehensive Package of Financial Reform

In any well-developed financial market, the supply and demand of each segment of the market affects that of other segments, thus constantly altering the rate structure, services, and size of each market, and eventually achieving allocating effects. It is becoming increasingly obvious that one single reform measure, such as introducing the function of the financial market, will not lead to a qualitative change in China's financial system. With restrictions on market participants, interest rates, and transfer of securities, financial markets, including money markets and capital markets, cannot fully play their roles as the markets themselves lack self-adjusting abilities to meet real supply and demand and are unrelated. Therefore, it is important for the Chinese government to conduct a comprehensive and coherent reform. In other words, the current institution-building in the banking sector and the development of the financial market should not be isolated experiments but should have a common theme. Also, the separate financial reform efforts should be solidified into a single comprehensive framework.

Properly Targeting the Priorities in Financial Market Development

Development of a financial sector is a complex undertaking. It is impossible to upgrade the system or make corrections or changes in a short period of time. Therefore, definition of a development strategy based on what is feasible and what is a priority is of crucial importance. For example, based on the current situation, it is more feasible to promote a corporate bond market than an equity market. However, the controls on interest rate ceilings and the differentiation of issuers need to be further improved before an active market can be developed.

Creating Conditions Favorable to Foreign Portfolio Investment

The investment requirements of China's modernization program promise to outpace China's traditional sources of funds, both internally and externally, by a significant margin. China has made significant efforts to attract direct foreign investment and has become active in international financial markets in order to raise the funds needed for its modernization program. Therefore, further efforts to create attractive conditions for introducing foreign portfolio investment through a number of investment vehicles should be made without delay in order to obtain another source of funding for development.

Unlike direct investment, most portfolio investment normally does not seek to take a controlling interest in the local company. Therefore, the issue of foreign control is negligible. To the extent that these additional funds allow more corporations to use equity financing, a more healthy corporate financial structure develops than is traditionally available. Finally, the use of equity rather than debt may also reduce the immediate debt-serving burden that foreign financing normally entails.

Foreign portfolio investment can also be an important supplement to the promotion of market maturity within the country. Therefore, China should seriously consider this option for attracting foreign funds. China has allowed limited foreign investment in its fledgling stock markets, and opened its Shanghai and Shenzhen markets to foreign investors in late 1991. A further opening of China's markets to mutual funds is anticipated in 1992. According to Wang Po-Ming, the vice president of China's Stock Exchange Executive Council, which oversees the new securities markets, a limited number of country funds will be allowed to invest. According to the same report, Hong Kong–based securities houses such as IndoSuez Asia, Barings, and Jardine Fleming have been waiting for openings on China's stock markets, but have not expected until recently to be admitted. When the situation becomes clearer, IndoSuez plans to launch a U.S. $20 million Shanghai fund.[4] More important at this point in time, however, is how to make the country attractive to foreign portfolio investment; that is, to ensure that the infrastructure necessary for a viable equity market is in place.

Establishing a Good Database System for Effective Control

Little attention has been paid thus far to the importance of a national and local database covering the development of securities markets in China. The lack of a good database and information system has made research difficult and will continue to handicap effective monitoring and control of the market as it develops. Modern technology has made a national information network much easier and China should take full advantage of this. The database should provide the information the questionnaire in this book attempted to obtain and the basic information that emerging markets in other countries present to the outside world.

NOTES

1. Michael Duckworth, "Foreigners Divided Over Chinese Stocks," *Asian Wall Street Journal*, January 17, 1992.

2. *Asian Wall Street Journal*, October 16, 1991, 6.

3. Ibid.

4. *Financial Times*, April 26, 1991.

Appendix I

Equity Markets in Economic Development

THE ROLE OF FINANCE IN DEVELOPMENT

Traditional economic and monetary theories have placed limited importance on financial development in comparison to other factors in the process of furthering economic development. Prior to the Great Depression of the 1930s, economists felt that monetary changes affected only prices and wages. Output and employment, the real factors in the economy, were considered to be independent of monetary events. Most economists believed that financial markets played largely a passive role in economic development.[1] The experience of the Great Depression made economists realize that monetary factors affected not only wages and prices but also changes in output and employment over the business cycle. For example, Keynes assigned some importance to the role of financial development by relating equilibrium in the money markets to general equilibrium in the economy as a whole.[2]

Since the early 1950s, ideas about the role of money in the development of an economy have undergone profound changes. Economists began examining money and finance from different perspectives with varying degrees of emphasis. The simple view that money is irrelevant to real growth and that accumulations of money retard real growth has been replaced by more complex considerations of the role of finance in general, including monetary and non-monetary financial instruments and their functions. Finance has been recognized as affecting not only the movement of the economy over the business cycle but also economic growth. Most economists abandoned the neoclassical economic notion that regarded the financial sector as neutral with respect to economic development. In the works of Edward S. Shaw, the financial sector of an economy does matter in economic development: it can assist in the break-away from the plodding repetition of repressed economic performance to accelerating growth and, if it is repressed and distorted, it can intercept and destroy impulses to development.[3] The disagreement, however, is still quite strong as to the cause and effect relationship between financial structure (i.e., the amalgamation of financial institutions, instruments, policies, markets regulations, and economic development).

Originally, the analysis of the effect of finance on growth was highly theoretical, couched in the language of the growth model. In a simple Harrod-Domar growth model, the increase in output is a function only of the rate at which physical capital is accumulated and the "efficiency" with which that capital is used.[4] Therefore, the growth in output is mainly a function of the savings rate (which is assumed to represent capital formation) and the capital output ratio. Thus a country that saves 20 percent of output and has an output-capital ratio of 0.25 would grow at 5 percent per year.

To ascertain the impact of money on growth, various writers modified the Harrod-Domar model by assuming that money is part of wealth and that the accumulation of money is an alternative for savers to accumulate physical assets. If the overall savings rate remains the same, the accumulation of additional money would reduce the accumulation of physical capital. As output depends only on physical capital, growth in physical output will slow as money is accumulated instead of physical capital. Thus if a country wishes to enhance the growth of physical output, it must slow the accumulation of money, which can be done by making the holding of money unattractive, say through inflation. Faulty assumptions in research and evaluation have added to the confusion about the contribution of finance to development. Many economists found this result both surprising and unacceptable and suggested different reasons why this simple approach might be misleading. One suggestion was that income should be more properly defined to include the services rendered by the money stock. Another suggestion was that money should be treated as a factor of production; more money would lead to more production.[5]

Of the various growth models with monetary aspects that emerged in the 1960s, the one that most clearly addressed the development problems was the modified growth model presented by Ronald I. McKinnon.[6] Investment, he assumed, was not perfectly divisible, but lumpy. Furthermore, people could not borrow to finance their investments; before making an investment, they had to accumulate purchasing power equal in value to the investment. In an economy without money, the accumulation of capital would be in the form of physical assets. If paper money were available, however, it could be substituted for physical assets, thus freeing resources for more productive purposes. McKinnon called this use of money the "conduit effect" and argued that to the extent that paper money was used to replace physical goods in capital accumulations, such an accumulation was a complement to physical capital accumulation, not a substitute. After all, the physical working balances had been replaced by paper money; further monetary accumulation would in McKinnon's model be an alternative to physical capital accumulation. Thus, there is a particular mix of a monetary system that maximizes growth.

The basic weakness in McKinnon's approach and, indeed, in similar models of the 1960s, is that they are concerned only with currency as against bank deposits, and so are of little help in understanding the conditions now found in developing countries. McKinnon's model gives insight into only two very particular situations. In the first, paper money replaced commodity money—say, gold or silver—thus freeing these physical resources for use in production. However, paper money has been used instead of commodity money for quite some time virtually everywhere except in some gold transactions in international trade. The second case to which McKinnon's analysis may apply is a hyperinflationary environment in which people have chosen not to hold fiat money and have shifted their liquid reserves into physical goods whose prices will appreciate with inflation. In this special case, there is a gain to be realized by increasing the use of money and by freeing the hoarded real resource for use in a productive purpose. McKinnon has made a small change in the neoclassical analysis that gives insight into the advantage of switching from commodity money to fiat money, but he has not presented a general model for understanding how finance affects economic growth.

Edward S. Shaw followed a different path to explain how finance affects growth.[7] He thought that money should be seen as only one of many financial assets, rather than being for singled out for special treatment. Shaw focused on the overall financial system, which, he argued, should be viewed as a service sector employing inputs to produce outputs. Essentially Shaw saw the service produced by the financial sector as intermediate input in the productive process. Producing more of that input would enhance the growth of real output. Shaw's approach is more useful than the growth models, however modified.

Inspired in large part by the works of McKinnon and Shaw, there has been a resurgence of interest in the role of financial development as a means of accelerating economic growth. Broadly speaking, two different schools of thought with somewhat different policy prescriptions can be identified. The first is the "financial structuralist" view, which maintains that a widespread network of financial institutions and a diversified array of financial instruments will have a beneficial effect on the saving-investment processes and hence on growth. The other is the "financial repressionist" view that considers low real interest rates, caused by arbitrarily set ceilings on nominal interest rates and high and variable inflation rates, as being the major impediments to financial deepening capital formation and growth. Thus, according to this school, the solution lies in allowing the interest rates to find their equilibrium levels in a free-market environment.

It was not until the early 1970s that economists and policy makers became concerned with the real-world applications of the theory of finance and growth, particularly with regard to developing countries. Numerous decentralized economies with low levels of per capita income and wealth have at times been attracted to a development strategy that results in "shallow" finance. Financial liberalization is rare because many reasons have been found for financial repression.[8] Shaw, among others, strongly advocated financial liberalization because: (a) financial liberalization tends to raise the ratio of private domestic savings into income; (b) liberalization permits the financial process of mobilizing and allocating savings to displace the fiscal process, inflation, and foreign aid to some degree; (c) liberalization opens the way to superior allocations of savings by widening and diversifying the financial markets in which investment opportunities compete for the savings flow and; (d) liberalization and allied policies tend to equalize the distribution of income and contribute to the stability of growth in output and employment.

THE FUNCTIONS OF A FINANCIAL SYSTEM

Assuming that financial development plays an important role in economic development, what services are provided by the financial sectors? Millard Long laid the groundwork for such analysis by suggesting some of the important functions performed by the financial sector.[9] The possible effects of the activities of financial intermediaries on the specific aspects or components of economic development, according to Millard Long, are divided into two broad categories: direct and indirect. Direct effects are defined as those that include the rate or amount of savings and/or investments. Indirect effects are all other effects of financial intermediaries on development, including the influences on such processes as encouraging private entrepreneurship, personnel training, redistribution of income, foreign exchange earnings, and transfer of technology.

The first and most basic function is the provision of a medium of exchange. Barter is clearly less efficient than monetized exchange. Although the use of money as a medium of exchange is taken for granted, Long argues that the benefits derived increase with the growth of specialization. However, "were this (referring to the provision of a medium of exchange) the only contribution of finance, a simple system would be adequate; all that would be required would be a central bank issuing paper money." Obviously, a financial system provides other services.[10]

The second function is more efficient allocation of investment. Good investment opportunities in an economy are not distributed among the same places and people as are the capacities to save. This theory rests on two assumptions: individual savers are not always the most efficient investors, and savers are not willing to make the full amount of their savings directly available to the most efficient investors. A well-functioning financial system mobilizes deposits from those savers with poor investment opportunities, performs the function of search and discrimination, and then allocates the available resources to those with higher-yielding investments.

Financial intermediation also provides incentives to investors. For many entrepreneurs, the increased availability of funds and financing flexibility as a result of financial intermediation may be considerably more significant than a reduction in costs. This is particularly true in developing countries where most markets are significantly less perfect than those in developed countries. Availability of funds from financial institutions enables the efficient entrepreneur to assume greater debt than otherwise possible and to engage in a larger amount of productive investment. Moreover, access to funds on reasonable terms from financial institutions can encourage entrepreneurs to expand their horizon of conceivable opportunities.

The third function is the provision of incentives to savings and growth. The development of a financial system and an associated provision of financial claims and services offers positive incentives for savings. Financial institutions stimulate savings by offering a wide array of financial assets. With increased availability of assets having higher yield, lower risk, and other durable characteristics, the return on savings is higher than before. With the trade-off between savings and present consumption becoming more favorable to the former, individuals save more. With the growth of financial intermediation, funds are channeled mainly to finance productive industrial and infrastructural investment. The resulting improvement in resource allocation raises the yield on capital and the level of output. In addition, if savings are responsive to the yield on capital, the overall increase in average yield should raise the economy's savings rate.

The fourth function is the transformation and distribution of risk. Most investors are risk-averse and must be reimbursed for bearing more risk. However, people differ in their tastes for risk. Some demand high compensation to bear risk, others less. A well-functioning financial system allocates risk to those who charge the least to bear it. A financial system can also transform risk in many ways. For example, in a project financed by both debt and equity, debt usually carries less risk than equity financing for the financier. Through financial intermediation, people can diversify their risk by having a minimal participation in many investments, rather than a large stake in just a few. Some kinds of risk are not shared but are actually reduced by a well-functioning financial system.

The final function, but not the least important, is the stabilization of an economy. All economies, at least market-oriented economies, experience cyclical changes in output and prices. This affects both the domestic economy and the balance of payments. When disturbances occur, governments employ countermeasures to stabilize economic activity. Today, financial policy is a common and usually a key stabilizing tool. The policies chosen depend in part on the nature of the disturbance. Through manipulation of the financial system, governments attempt to keep both the domestic economy and the country's foreign position in balance.

FINANCIAL DEVELOPMENT AND ECONOMIC DEVELOPMENT

There is no precise definition available in the literature as to the meaning of financial development. Raymond W. Goldsmith de-

fined financial development as "changes in financial structure."[11]
As to the relationship between financial development and economic development, Goldsmith made the following observations:

> In general, financial development proceeds concomitantly with
> economic development, with finance playing an increasingly im-
> portant role. With growth of real per capita output, an economy
> passes through sequential phases of financial development, first the
> monetization of economic activities as substance production and
> barter give way to commercialization, then the development of
> commercial banking as the main source of increased financial
> claims, and finally the relative growth of thrift and other specialized
> long-term financial institutions. Primitive economies have very
> limited and simple financial systems, consisting only of some
> rudimentary form of money such as beads or metal. Modern,
> developed countries have highly complicated and differentiated
> financial structures, consisting of thousands of different types of
> financial instruments and institutions, with complex patterns of
> ownership and regulation of institutions and markets.[12]

He concludes that: "This is the single major path of financial
development on which all countries will or have passed, a path
countries have travelled at different speeds, and a path they have
deviated from only to a minor extent."[13]

Goldsmith and others have been using the financial interrela-
tions ratio as an indicator of financial deepening. This ratio is
defined as the ratio of a set of financial assets to total wealth, which
was determined by a country's per capita income, its rate of growth,
and the actual rate of inflation. In practice, however, a narrower
definition, in which the numerator generally is M1 or M2 and the
denominator is the GNP, has been used. The broader definition is
preferable if data availability allows its usage.

However, there are differences in national financial systems that
cannot be explained by differences in income and wealth. The
principal reason of dissimilar financial structures at similar levels
of national income and wealth, Shaw argues, is the presence of

alternative techniques for mobilizing economic surplus, for eliciting savings and allocating them to investment. He stated,

> Economic development is marked by iterative proving for the optimal combination of savings-investment technologies. The search is guided in part by principle and prejudice, in part by foreign example, by trial and error, and even by rational analysis. The combinations and permutations of savings-investment technology are so numerous that no two countries are likely to follow the same probing sequence or, specifically, to reach the same ratio of financial assets to tangible wealth at any given level of real wealth or income per capita.[14]

Goldsmith also concludes that if one dared to suggest a Law of Financial Development, it would be this:

> Each economy begins its development by intensive exploration of a saving-investment technology that is chosen for historical, political, social or perhaps economic reasons, and then, as this technology produces a diminishing net yield, experiments with alternative technology that are marginally superior in terms of their capitalized returns and costs begin. Whatever the first choice may be, it is tilled intensively until there is an obvious advantage in trying a new mix of processes for eliciting and allocating savings.

In addition to these arguments, there is also a concept of "demand-following" and "supply-leading" in "supply-leading finance" development theory introduced by Hugh T. Patrick.[15] The term "demand-following" refers to the creation of modern financial institutions, their financial assets and liabilities, and related financial services in response to the demand for these services by investors and savers in the real economy. In this case, the evolution of the financial system is a consequence of economic development.

Patrick argues that the nature of the demand for financial services depends on the growth of total output and on the commercialization and monetization of agriculture and other traditional sectors. The more rapid the growth rate of real national income, the greater will be the demand of enterprises for external funds and, therefore, for financial intermediation. The greater the variance in growth rates among different sectors or industries, the greater the need for financial intermediation to transfer savings to fast-growing industries from elsewhere in the economy. The "demand-following" approach implies that finance is essentially passive. In this view, the lack of financial institutions in developing countries indicates the lack of demand for their services.

"Supply-leading" finance means creating financial institutions and instruments in advance of demand for them in an effort to stimulate economic growth. The major function of "supply-leading" finance is to promote and stimulate entrepreneurial responses. Access to "supply-leading" financial services opens new horizons, enabling entrepreneurs to "think big." Moreover, the top management of financial institutions may also serve as entrepreneurs. They may assist in the establishment of firms in new industries or in the merger of firms by underwriting a substantial portion of the capital and by assuming the entrepreneurial initiative. "Supply-leading" phenomena represent a situation in which financial development causes economic development. The success of "supply-leading" finance, however, appears to depend on government support, cautious experimentation, public confidence, and relatively stable prices.

Patrick also suggests that both phenomena may exist at different stages of development. He argues that it cannot be said that supply-leading finance is a necessary condition or precondition for self-sustained economic development; rather, it represents an opportunity to induce real growth by financial means. In practice, there is likely to be an interaction of "supply-leading" and "demand-following" phenomena. The following sequence may be postulated:

Before sustained modern industrial growth gets under way, "supply-leading" finance may be able to induce real innovation. As the process of real growth occurs, the "supply-leading" impetus becomes less important, and the "demand-following" financial response becomes dominant. This shift is also likely to occur within and among specific industries or sectors at different phases of their growth.[16]

In summary, where does modern thinking now stand on the financial side of the economy? First, economists no longer consider money merely a variable that affects only prices and not output. Rather, they understand that finance affects production, not only over the business cycle but also in the longer course of economic development. Second, economists no longer conceive of money as providing only a medium of exchange. Rather, they realize that exchange is only one of several key services provided by the financial system. Third, the debate is no longer limited to the behavior of banks and their key liability deposits. Economists and policy makers are now thinking about the role of the whole financial system and the entirety of financial assets. However, since this is a recent development, there is still much to learn about the relationship between overall economic conditions and the performance of the financial system.

THE ROLE OF EQUITY MARKETS IN DEVELOPMENT

Raising funds for investment in long-term assets is often regarded as the primary if not the only economic contribution of equity markets to economic development. This narrow view ignores the other important contributions that an equity market can make. From the works of Antoine W. van Agtmael, P. J. Drake, U. Tun Wai, and Hugh T. Patrick, these benefits can be summarized as follows.[17]

Better Resource Allocation

Effective equity markets force corporations to compete on an equal basis for the funds of investors and open horizons for entrepreneurs. Without securities markets, companies have to rely on

internal financing through retained earnings. Well-established enterprises are in a privileged position because they can make investments
from retained earnings while new companies do not have easy access
to such financing. Without being subjected to the scrutiny of the
marketplace, big firms get bigger. Corporate ownership and decision-making thus remains in the hands of a few. New ideas may not
be tried and a country's technology may gradually become obsolete.
Therefore, the efficient allocation of plant, equipment and working
capital in firms in the economy depends on the efficiency with which
financial capital is distributed. The amount of funds a firm seeks to
raise by the sale of securities depends on the profitability with which
the fund can be used.

In economies with heavy government intervention, healthy
equity markets can also serve as a safety valve to ensure that the
distortions created by planning and other forms of government
intervention do not become too great. It is very questionable
whether small groups of central planners or bankers can make
better judgments, in the long run, in allocating investment than
decentralized market forces can.

More Competitive and Solvent Financial System

The existence of an active market for equities and other securities creates alternatives to the banking system for both savers and
users of funds. Savers can compare the yield of equity (or bonds)
with the interest rate on deposits, and companies can compare the
cost of various sources of financing. In many countries there is not
enough competition within the banking system; other bank-type
institutions do not exist or are unable to compete effectively. The
existence of an equity market can serve to make the financial
system more competitive and efficient. Securities compete with
bank deposits that may be subject to interest rate controls. This
exerts pressure to keep the "controlled" interest rates closer to
"market" rates that are more likely to reflect inflation and scarcity
of funds.

Equally important is the potential contribution of securities markets to the solvency of the financial system. The absence of viable equity markets tends to increase the debt/equity ratios of corporations, weakening their capital structure. This endangers not only their long-term viability but also the solvency of their lenders in the banking system.

Solvency of the Corporate Sector

The macroeconomic arguments for equity markets have received more attention from policymakers and economists than the potential impacts of securities and especially equity markets at the "corporate" level. At the microlevel, benefits for corporations include:

1. Stronger corporate balance sheet: Healthy debt/equity ratios are a major underlying requirement for a robust economic system. In the absence of an efficient equity market, debt/equity ratios inevitably rise.
2. Improved access to financing for new and emerging companies: In several countries, the equity market plays an important role in directly raising risk capital for new and emerging companies. Venture capitals usually thrive best in an active securities market environment.
3. Easier owner/non-owner management transition: The existence of a marketplace provides a price as well as buyers, making it easier for founders of companies to sell out and leave the business to professional management.
4. Better management information: The need for disclosure of financial information is a strong incentive for the improvement of internal financial information.

However, despite all the benefits derived from a healthy equity market, the development of such a market also involves risks and costs if not properly set up and regulated. There are certain problems inherent in the system that cannot be avoided, such as

the inevitability of market cycles, possibilities of speculation, and
dishonest activities and, therefore, the need for additional regulation. Loss of some control over the financial system is also possible.

Wall Street in the late 1920s, Hong Kong in 1973, and the
unofficial Sook Almanakh in Kuwait in 1982 are three striking
examples of stock markets encouraging speculation both by individuals and institutions. Stock markets provide an arena for dishonest activity, such as conflict of interest, market rigging, insider
trading, and the issuing of false or misleading prospectus.

In many countries, the financial system is composed only of
banks or other similar institutions. Investment financing basically
occurs through direct control of the granting or withholding of
credit to public and private institutions. With the establishment of
equity markets, there is less direct control over the countries'
financial systems. The benefits and costs of an equity market must
therefore be viewed in light of the goals and objectives of the total
financial system, rather than in isolated components. Equity markets are an important part of a country's financial system but are
not the only part. Although it may be necessary to emphasize equity
markets during a particular period of financial system development, equity market development should always be viewed as part
of a balanced financial system and as a means toward other, more
fundamental economic and social policy objectives.

REQUIREMENTS FOR A SUCCESSFUL EQUITY MARKET

Equity market development is often regarded as an important
part of the financial development process and an important indicator of financial deepening. It is often considered as part of the
latter stage in the financial development of a country. Some regard
equity market development as an evolutionary process correlated
to per capita income. Environments supportive of equity markets
have various dimensions, such as the development of both the
economic and financial system. "It does not make sense to rely on

equity markets for resource mobilization and allocation in an economy with a low per capita income and weak institutional structure," Wai and Patrick argue.[18] A key question therefore has been raised: are equity markets necessary for all countries regardless of their stage of economic development? The basic prerequisites for the establishment and continued success of an equity market as summarized by Antoine W. van Agtmael contain the following elements.[19]

A Reasonably Stable Political Environment

Investors, particularly equity investors, are very sensitive to political uncertainty. In countries that are in domestic turmoil, major border conflicts, or a war, there is little possibility of establishing a stock market and attracting investment in any kind of long-term securities. If a market exists, trading activity and prices are usually in a decline. Political disruption nearly always affects economic activities and undermines investors' confidence in economic stability and growth.

A Healthy Economic Environment

The level of economic development usually determines whether there is a sufficient demand for and supply of equities. Not having enough stocks to trade adequately is often a greater constraint on the development of an active market than the number of investors in developing countries. Factors influencing the supply of securities include: (a) the size of the economy, its level of development, its growth rate, and, therefore, its need for a sizable amount of additional capital; (b) a free-enterprise orientation that largely determines the number of sizable corporations that are qualified and likely to list their stocks on the exchange; (c) the attitude of existing owners of the company toward allowing outsiders into the company; and (d) the interest policies, tax policies, and other inducements of the government.

The demand for stocks and other securities depends on another set of factors: (a) the number of financially sophisticated individuals with enough money to purchase securities; (b) institutional demand, which is the demand from insurance companies, pension funds, or mutual funds; (c) the attractiveness of securities, including stocks, compared to other investment alternatives and; (d) the rule of foreign portfolio investment, which may be significant or may be actively discouraged.

Economies dominated by government-owned enterprises (as in many socialist and African countries) or those with scarce entrepreneurial experience are not likely candidates for the establishment of an equity market, based on the reasons listed above. An exception may arise when the government of these countries has made a conscious decision to change course and to sell its stake in government corporations and allow them to be run on a private-enterprise basis.

A Favorable Policy Environment

The government's attitude and policies directly influence the supply of and demand for financial instruments, particularly equity shares. The mobilization of long-term domestic savings also depends on sound fiscal, monetary, and investor policies and practices. Unfavorable or unstable macroeconomic policies (for example, high inflation, negative real interest rates, frequent devaluations, and discriminatory tax treatment of investment) are major reasons for the lack of activity of securities markets in many developing countries. Based on the experience of these developing countries, the following aspects are seen as critical to the success of equity markets:

1. Some willingness to rely on market forces rather than solely on central planning;
2. A favorable government attitude and an economic structure in which private enterprises are allowed to play a significant role;

3. Non-discriminatory tax treatment of investments of all kind with some special temporary tax and other incentives for high-risk investments;

4. An adequate legal framework, including protection of outside investors through securities legislation and its enforcement;

5. Reasonably well-developed accounting and auditing standards.

In summary, equity markets are greatly affected by political, economic, and legal factors. Without the above-mentioned environment, a viable equity market cannot develop; it will either remain dormant or be subjected to excessive speculation. It is obvious that these factors are closely related to the level of economic development a country has achieved and the type of development path it has chosen.

NOTES

1. Millard Long, "A Note on Financial Theory and Economic Development," *Contribution of Finance to Development* (Washington, D.C.: World Bank Publications, 1985), 23.

2. John Maynard Keynes, *The General Theory of Employment, Interest and Money* (New York: Harcourt Brace, 1936).

3. Edward S. Shaw, *Financial Deepening in Economic Development* (New York: Oxford University Press, 1973), 3.

4. Long, "A Note on Financial Theory and Economic Development," 23.

5. Ibid., 24.

6. Ronald I. McKinnon, *Money and Capital in Economic Development* (Washington, D.C.: Brookings Institution, 1973).

7. Shaw, *Financial Deepening in Economic Development*, 3.

8. Shaw suggested some of the reasons: The first is the historic antipathy to usury. Second, effective control has not been established over ratios of growth in nominal money and rates of change in price levels. Third, various models of aggregate economic behavior, which are applied to economic policy, minimize or misinterpret the role of finance, and finally, the results of real financial growth are not worth the

costs involved and that alternative solutions of capital scarcity are superior.

9. Long, "A Note on Financial Theory and Economic Development," 22–28.

10. Ibid., 26.

11. Raymond W. Goldsmith, *Financial Structure and Development* (New Haven: Yale University Press, 1969), 11.

12. Ibid., 26–29.

13. Ibid., 30.

14. Ibid., 58.

15. Hugh T. Patrick, "Financial Development and Economic Growth in Underdeveloped Countries," *Economic Development and Cultural Change* (January 1966), 174–189.

16. Ibid., 184.

17. Antoine W. van Agtmael, *Emerging Securities Markets* (EUROMONEY Publications, 1984); P. J. Drake, "Securities Markets in Less Developed Countries," *Journal of Developmental Studies* (January 1977), 72–91; U. Tung Wai and Hugh T. Patrick, "Stock and Bond Issues and Capital Markets in Less Developed Countries," International Monetary Fund Staff Papers: *Capital Market in Less Developed Countries* (1973), 255–317.

18. U. Tun Wai and Hugh T. Patrick, "Stock and Bond Issues," 268.

19. Van Agtmael, *Emerging Securities Markets*.

Appendix II

A Survey on Bond and Stock Issuances in China

APPENDIX II

Part I: General Survey

1.   Name of enterprise: _____

   _____

2.   Line of business:

   Heavy industry   _____

   Light industry   _____

   High-tech industry   _____

   A combination of the above   _____

   Others (please specify)   _____

   _____

   3.   Main products or services (please list one or more):

   (1)   _____

   (2)   _____

   (3)   _____

   (4)   _____

4.   Type of ownership:

   State-owned   _____

   Collectively-owned   _____

   Joint-stock   _____

   Private owned   _____

   Others (please specify)   _____

   _____

5.   Name of employees at present: _____

6.   Number of years in operation:

     1-5 _____

     6-10 _____

     11-20 _____

     21-30 _____

     31 or more _____

7.   Current Total Assets (in RMB): _____

8.   Total assets in the past five years (in RMB): _____

     1983 _____

     1984 _____

     1985 _____

     1986 _____

     1987 _____

9.   Total output in the past five years (in RMB):

     1983 _____

     1984 _____

     1985 _____

     1986 _____

     1987 _____

10. Generally speaking, total output in the past five years has

     Substantially increased _____

     Increased _____

     Had some ups and downs _____

Decreased   _____

Substantially decreased   _____

11.   Total net earnings in the past five years:

      1983   _____

      1984   _____

      1985   _____

      1986   _____

      1987   _____

12.   Generally speaking, total earnings in the past five years has

      Substantially increased   _____

      Increased   _____

      Had some ups and downs   _____

      Decreased   _____

      Substantially decreased   _____

13.   Source of funds in the past three years and the percentage of each if known:

	1985	1986	1987
State investment allocation	____	____	____ %
Bank loans	____	____	____ %
Bonds and stocks	____	____	____ %
Retained earnings	____	____	____ %
Others (please specify)	____	____	____ %

14.   Generally speaking, the funds for the following sources have increased/decreased
      (please check one per category):

      State Budget allocation   increased   _____   decreased   _____

Bank loans	increased	_____	decreased	_____
Bonds and stocks	increased	_____	decreased	_____
Retained earnings	increased	_____	decreased	_____

15. How would you rate the need to raise funds by issuing stocks and bonds?

Very urgent _____   Fairly urgent _____   Not urgent _____

Part II: Bond Issuing Activities

1. When did your enterprise first issue bonds?

   1984 _____

   1985 _____

   1986 _____

   1987 _____

   1988 _____

2. How many issuances have you made since then and what was the amount of each issuance?

	Year of issuance	Total amount (in RMB)
1st	_____	_____
2nd	_____	_____
3rd	_____	_____

3. Did you have other financing alternatives when you issued bonds?

   Yes _____   No _____

   If yes, what were they?

   State capital allocation   _____

   Bank loans   _____

   Others (please specify)   _____

4.   If you had other financing alternatives, you chose to raise funds by issuing bonds because (please check one or more)

    (a)   Funding from other sources was not enough   _____

    (b)   The cost of capital was lower when issuing bonds   _____

    (c)   The enterprise wanted to experiment with this new way of raising capital even though the cost was a little bit higher than other alternatives   _____

5.   Generally speaking, what percentage did the funds raised through issuing bonds account for in the total financing needs of the past few years?

    5-10%   _____

    11-15%   _____

    16-20%   _____

    More than 20%   _____

6.   What were the denominations of the bonds in RMB (please check one or more):

    10 _____   20 _____   30 _____

    50 _____   100 _____   over 100 _____

7.   What were the maturities of the bonds?

	1st issue	2nd issue	3rd issue
1-2 years	_____	_____	_____
3-5 years	_____	_____	_____
6-10 years	_____	_____	_____
10 years	_____	_____	_____

8.   What were the interest rates?

    1st issue   _____

2nd issue   _____

3rd issue   _____

9. Were your bonds sold at face value or at discount?

At face value   _____

At discount   _____

If at discount, what was the discount rate?   _____

10. Did you sell your bonds directly or through banks?

Directly by ourselves   _____

Through banks   _____

11. To whom were the primary issues sold and if possible, give the percentage of each:

Individuals   _____%

Own employees   _____%

Other enterprises _____%

Banks   _____%

Others (please specify)   _____

_____%

Why were the bonds sold to the ones you have indicated rather than to others?

Please explain: _____

_____

_____

12. What are the main purpose of issuing bonds (please check one or more)?

(a) To expand existing production facility   _____

(b) For technical renovations   _____

(c) To start a new business   _____

(d)   To start a new venture with a foreign firm   _____

(e)   To make up a working capital shortage   _____

(f)   Others (please specify)   _____

_____

13.   Are your bonds traded on the secondary market?

        Yes _____   No _____

14.   How did you feel about raising funds by issuing bonds compared with borrowing

        from banks?

        Easy   _____

        Complicated   _____

        More beneficial   _____

        Less beneficial   _____

15.   Are you free to issue bonds whenever it is necessary and for whatever project needs

        financing?

        Yes _____   No _____

16.   Are you restricted on the amount of bonds you can issue?

        Yes _____   No _____

17.   Based on your past experience, would you like to issue bonds again?

        Yes _____   No _____

        If yes, please explain: _____

        _____

        _____

        _____

        If no, please explain: _____

_____

_____

_____

18.   I would appreciate it if you could send me a copy of the prospectus of the bond issuance.

Part III: Stock Issuing Activities

1.   When did you first issue stocks?

    1984   _____

    1985   _____

    1986   _____

    1987   _____

    1988   _____

2.   How many times have you issued stocks since the first issuance?

    Once   _____

    Twice   _____

    Three times or more   _____

3.   What is the total number of shares currently outstanding?   _____

4.   Equity accounts for what percentage of your total assets?

    Less than 10%   _____

    11-25%   _____

    26-35%   _____

    More than 35%   _____

5.   What was the total amount of capital raised?

    1st issue   _____   RMB

2nd issue   _____   RMB

3rd issue   _____   RMB

6.   What was the prior per share?

1st issue   _____   RMB

2nd issue   _____   RMB

3rd issue   _____   RMB

7.   What were the purposes of issuing stocks (please check one or more)?

(a)   To expand existing production facility   _____

(b)   For technical renovation   _____

(c)   To start a new operation   _____

(d)   To start a new venture with a foreign firm   _____

(e)   To make up working capital shortage   _____

(f)   As an attempt to improve management   _____

(g)   As an attempt to change enterprise ownership _____

(h)   Others (please specify) _____

       _____

8.   Did you have other financing alternatives when you issued stocks?

             Yes _____   No _____

      If yes, what were they?

(a)   Bank loans   _____

(b)   State capital allocation   _____

(c)   Issuing bonds   _____

(d)   Others (please specify) _____

       _____

9.   If you had other financing alternatives, why did you issue stocks?

(a)   Funding from other sources was not enough   _____

(b)   It was more beneficial to the operation of the enterprise   _____

(c)   Wanted to experiment with this new way of raising capital   _____

10.   Generally speaking, what percentage did the funds raised through issuing stocks account for in total financing needs of the past few years?

5-10%   _____

11-15%   _____

16-20%   _____

More than 20%   _____

11.   To whom were the stocks sold, and what was the percentage of each?

(a)   Individuals   _____

(b)   Own employees   _____

(c)   Other enterprises   _____

(d)   Banks   _____

(e)   Others (please specify)   _____

12.   If the stocks were sold only to your own employees, what were the reasons (please check one or more)?

(a)   The total number of shares was limited   _____

(b)   The enterprise was not well known   _____

(c)   It was easier to manage the issuance   _____

(d)   Could not meet the requirements for issuing to the public   _____

(e)   Wanted to sell to own employees as a trial first. If
       successful, would sell to the public in the future   _____

    (f)   Others (please specify)   _____

13.   You sold stocks to the public because:

    (a)   The number of shares was large   _____

    (b)   The enterprise was well-established and well-known

           to the public   _____

    (c)   The requirements of the public issuance were not stringent

           and could be met by smaller enterprises   _____

    (d)   It was more interesting to sell stocks to the public

           than to own employees only   _____

14.   Did you sell stocks directly or through banks?

          Directly _____   Through banks _____

15.   How do you pay dividends?

    (a)   According to the enterprise performance profits _____

    (b)   Certain interest rate plus dividends   _____

    (c)   Fixed amount of interest rate   _____

    (d)   Other ways (please specify)   _____

16.   How often do you pay dividends?

    Quarterly   _____

    Semi-annually   _____

    Annually   _____

    Not regularly   _____

    Other ways (please specify)   _____

17.   What were the approximate returns on your stocks for the past few years?

(a)   Below 5%   _____

(b)   6-10%   _____

(c)   11-15%   _____

(d)   16-20%   _____

(e)   Above 20%   _____

18.   Are you restricted by any upper limit on the stock dividends you can pay?

         Yes _____   No _____

       If yes, what are the restrictions? _____

       _____

19.   Do you hold shareholder meetings regularly?

         Yes _____   No _____

       If yes, how often? _____

20.   What are the main issues discussed at shareholder meetings?

       _____

       _____

       _____

21.   How do you feel about raising capital by issuing stocks compared with issuing bonds
       or obtaining bank loans?

       (a)   Easy   _____

       (b)   Complicated   _____

       (c)   More beneficial _____

       (d)   Less beneficial _____

22.   Based on your past experience, do you plan to make further issuances again?

         Yes _____   No _____

If yes, why?

_____

_____

_____

If no, why?

_____

_____

_____

23.   Do you feel pressure to improve management and profitability so that you can have
       better terms for your enterprise when you issue stocks and/or bonds?

       Very much so _____ Not so much _____ Not at all _____

24.   Are your stocks traded on the secondary market?

                    Yes _____   No _____

Part IV: Trading of Bonds and Stocks

1.   What kinds of securities are traded on your trading center right now? Please give
       the approximate percentage of each.

       (a)   Treasury bills   _____ %

       (b)   Corporate bonds   _____ %

       (c)   Financial bonds   . _____ %

       (d)   Municipal bonds   _____ %

       (e)   Corporate stocks   _____ %

2.   What do you require for listing on your trading center?

       (a)   _____

       (b)   _____

(c) _____

(d) _____

3.   What is the average trading volume per day?

(a)   1-20 transactions   _____

(b)   21-40 transactions   _____

(c)   41-60 transactions   _____

(d)   61-80 transactions   _____

(e)   81 or more   _____

4.   Please grade the trading activities of the following securities on your trading center

as:

	Very Active	Active	Less Active
Treasury bills	_____	_____	_____
Corporate bonds	_____	_____	_____
Financial bonds	_____	_____	_____
Municipal bonds	_____	_____	_____
Corporate stocks	_____	_____	_____

5.   Can you give reasons why certain securities are more actively traded than others?

(a)   Frequent price movement makes the security profitable to trade   _____

(b)   The total amount of the security when first issued was big   _____

(c)   Easiness to have the transaction done   _____

(d)   Particular features of the security attract investors' interest   _____

6.   Do you allow free fluctuation of price?

Yes _____   No _____   Only to some extent _____

7.   What affects the fluctuation of price most?

(a)   Bank interest rates   _____

(b)   Performance of enterprise   _____

(c)   Demand and supply of the security   _____

8.   What is the approximate range of price fluctuations?

Very small   _____

Occasional ups and downs   _____

Relatively volatile   _____

9.   What king of stock performs better than others on your trading center (please list one or two)?

(a)   _____

(b)   _____

10.   Do you have some idea why holders sell their stocks?

Take profit   _____

Need cash   _____

Exchange for other stocks or bonds   _____

11.   What is the average transaction amount for an individual?

100-300 RMB   _____

301-500 RMB   _____

501-800 RMB   _____

800-over RMB   _____

12.   Are you aware of some frequent players, i.e. those who trade his or her stocks and bonds frequently?

Yes _____   No _____

13.   How difficult is it to complete a transaction?

Very difficult   _____

Fairly difficult   _____

Not difficult   _____

14.   What are the major difficulties in trading?

Not enough sellers   _____

Not enough buyers   _____

Regulations on price movement   _____

Poor facilities to execute orders   _____

Not familiar with the trading business yet   _____

15.   Do you allow institutions to trade blocks of shares on your trading center?

          Yes _____   No _____

16.   Does institutions' buying and selling happen frequently?

          Yes _____   No _____

17.   What measures do you consider most important to increase trading activities?

More listings of bonds and stocks   _____

Better communications facilities   _____

More legal protection for investors   _____

Allowing prices to move freely   _____

18.   The stocks and bonds that are traded represent only a tiny proportion of the stocks

       and bonds issued. What factors prevent them from being traded?

       Enterprises are not performing well enough to be listed on

       trading centers   _____

       The number is purposely kept small at this experimental stage   _____

19.   How many employees work in your trading center?   _____

20.   Do you have any plan to expand trading activities and/or to separate
      trading of debt securities and stocks in the near future?

      Yes _____   No _____   See how market develops _____

21.   What is your single most important recommendation to further improve the
      environment for the development of securities markets in China?

      _____

      _____

      _____

Appendix III

Interim Regulations on the Administration of Bonds of Enterprises

Promulgated by the State Council on 27 March 1987
CHAPTER 1
General Principles

Article 1

The present Regulations are formulated with a view to strengthening the administration of bonds of enterprises, guiding the rational channeling of capital, effectively exploiting the scattered capital of the community, ensuring the construction of key projects by the state, and protecting the lawful rights of the various parties.

Article 2

The present Regulations apply to bonds issued by the enterprises owned by the whole people within the PRC which are qualified as legal persons.

Article 3

The issue and purchase of bonds of enterprises shall comply with the principles of voluntariness, mutual benefit, and compensation of equal value.

The issue of bonds of enterprises by designated allocation is strictly prohibited.

Article 4

The People's Bank of China is the authority in charge of the issue of bonds of enterprises and its approval shall be obtained prior to issuing bonds.

CHAPTER II
Bonds of Enterprises

Article 5

Bonds of enterprises are issued by enterprise through the statutory process and repayable with the due interest within a specified time.

Article 6

The following contents of the bonds shall be stated at par:

(1) The name and address of the enterprise;

(2) The par value of the bond;

(3) The par interest rate of the bond;

(4) The term and form of maturity;

(5) The form of interest payment;

(6) The date of issue of the bond and the serial number;

(7) The seal of the issuing enterprise and the endorsement of the statutory representative; and

(8) The official serial number and date of approval by the authority of examination and approval.

Article 7

The format of the bonds shall be subject to the approval of the People's Bank of China.

Article 8

The holder of the bonds is entitled to receive interest and be repaid the principal in a fixed period of time, but he shall not have any role in the management of the enterprise.

Article 9

The holder of the bonds shall not be held liable to the state of the business.

Article 10

Bonds may be assigned, or taken as security or inherited.

Article 11

An enterprise may, based on the characteristics and market demands for the invested item, issue bonds which are repayable by its products of equal value, provided approval has been obtained.

CHAPTER III
The Administration of Bonds of Enterprises

Article 12

The quota of nationwide bonds of enterprises to be issued shall be formulated by the People's Bank of China in consultation with the department of state planning and finance, and shall be dispatched to all provinces, autonomous regions, municipalities, and listed cities of the provinces for enforcement.

Article 13

The People's Bank of China shall exercise centralized administration on the issuing of bonds by enterprises but its examination and approval shall be delegated to various levels.

Article 14

An enterprise shall announce the rules and procedures for the issue of bonds. The rules and procedures shall include the following content: operational and managerial conditions of the enterprise in brief; net value of the self-owned assets; objectives of issuing bonds; forecast of results; total value of bonds; form of repayment of principal and interest; and responsibility of risks.

Article 15

The applicant enterprise shall forward the following documents to the People's Bank of China or its branch organizations:

(1) the application form for issuing bonds;

(2) business license;

(3) the papers of approval for the issue of bonds from the appropriate authority;

(4) the papers of approval from the department of planning on the fixed asset investment;

(5) the rules and procedures for the issue of bonds;

(6) the financial and accounting reports of the past two years and the immediate past quarter of the enterprise as duly endorsed by the proper competent authority or by the accounting firm; and

(7) other information requested by the People's Bank of China.

Article 16

The total value of bonds issued by an enterprise shall not exceed the total net value of the assets owned by itself.

Article 17

An enterprise issues bonds for investing in fixed assets. Its investments shall be subject to the examination and approval of the relevant departments and shall be included in the limit of fixed asset investments under control.

Article 18

The interest rate of the bonds shall not exceed 40% of the interest rate payable by the banks to the citizens on their fixed savings deposits for the same duration.

Article 19

In the purchase of bonds, an enterprise owned by the whole people may only deploy the capital approved by the state with the right of independent allocation.

In the purchase of bonds, a business organization may only deploy the capital approved by the state with the right of independent allocation.

Article 20

Tax shall be levied on the interest earned by organizations or individuals from the bonds of enterprises.

Article 21

An enterprise may issue the bonds by itself or entrust a bank or other financial institution to issue the bonds on its behalf.

The agency which issues bonds on entrustment shall collect a certain rate of handling charge proportionate to the total value of bonds issued.

The agency which issues bonds on entrustment shall not bear any liability for the state of business of the issuing organization.

Article 22

Subject to the approval of the People's Bank of China, all specialized banks or other financial institutions may engage in the business of assignment of bonds.

Article 23

Non-financial institutions or citizens shall not engage in the issue of bonds through agency or assignment of the same.

Article 24

The People's Bank of China shall have the right to inspect and supervise the use of capital in the bond issuing enterprises and in all enterprises and organizations engaging in the purchase of bonds.

CHAPTER IV
Legal Liabilities

Article 25

The People's Bank of China or its branch organizations may impose the following penalties on the bond issuing enterprise for any breach against Articles 3 (paragraph 2), 4, 7, 11, 15 and 17:

(1) it shall be ordered to stop the illegal activities and refund all the capital raised;

(2) the funds raised from the issue of bonds shall be frozen;

(3) to inform the financial institution with which the enterprise has an account to stop the credit facilities; and

(4) a fine of not more than 5% of the amount involved in the illegal activity.

The above penalties may be executed simultaneously.

Article 26

The People's Bank of China or its branch organizations may impose the following penalties on any financial institution, non-financial institution or individual citizen found to be in breach of Articles 22 and 23;

(1) it or he shall be ordered to stop the illegal business;
(2) the illegal proceeds shall be forfeited; and
(3) a fine of not more than 5% of the amount involved in the illegal activities.

The above penalties may be executed simultaneously.

Article 27

The responsible officials of organizations which have been penalized by Articles 26 and 27 of the present Regulations shall be subject to investigation of their administrative and economic liabilities.

Article 28

Any official in the department in charge of bond issuing enterprises who has been found to be in breach of the present Regulations, or negligent of duties or guilty of corrupt practice shall be subject to administrative and economic sanctions.

CHAPTER V
Supplementary Provisions

Article 29

The interpretation of the present Regulations resides with the People's Bank of China which shall also formulate the detailed rules of implementation.

Article 30

The present Regulations shall come into force on the day of promulgation.

Bibliography

Anckonie, Alex, and Chang-hyun Chi. "Internationalization of the Korean Stock Market." Paper presented at the Korean Economic Institute of America Meeting, November 1986.

Basseer, Potkin. "The Role of Financial Intermediation in Economic Development: The Case of Iran, 1978–1988." *DBA Dissertation*, George Washington University, 1982.

Bian, Fa. "Reform—China's Second Revolution." *China Reconstructs* (October 1987): 16–20.

Black, Harold, William Darity, and Bobbie Lee Horn. "Financial Intermediation and Economic Development: A Survey of Theoretical and Empirical Work and Policy Issues." *World Bank*, 1985.

Brothman, Daniel. "Reforming the Domestic Banking System." *The China Business Review* (March–April 1985): 17–23.

Calamanti, Andrea. *The Securities Market and Underdevelopment: The Stock Exchange in the Ivory Coast, Morocco and Tunisia.* Milan: Giuffra, 1983.

Canto, Jorje Del. "Impact of Inflation on the Development of Capital Markets in Argentina and Brazil." *Capital Markets Under Inflation*, Nicholas Bruck, ed. Stock Exchange of Buenos Aires, Argentina (1982): 119–189.

Calvo, Guillermo, and Jacob Frenkel. "From Centrally-Planned to Market Economies: The Road from CPE to PCPE." *Working Paper*, WP/91/17, International Monetary Fund, 1991.

Chen, Muhua. "Structural Reforms Promote Trade." *Intertrade* (January 1985): 8–10.

Cheng, Hang-Sheng. "Financial Deepening in Pacific Basin Countries."
    Economic Review, Federal Reserve Bank of San Francisco,
    Summer 1980.
"China Marches to a Changing Turn." *EUROMONEY* (August 1990):
    47–50.
"China's Stock Market—Born Again?" *The China Business Review*
    (January–February 1986): 37.
Chuppe, Terry, and Hugh Haworth. "Public Policy Toward the Interna-
    tional Bond Activities in the 1980s." *United States Securities
    and Exchange Commission*, February 1988.
————. "The Securities Markets in the 1980s: A Global Perspective."
    United States Securities and Exchange Commission, January
    1989.
de Costa, Roberto Teixeira. "Capital Market in Brazil: Analysis of
    Performance and Outlook." *Capital Markets Under Inflation*,
    Nicholas Bruck, ed. Stock Exchange of Buenos Aires, Argen-
    tina (1982): 39–72.
————. *Brazil's Experience in Creating a Capital Market*. Transla-
    tion by Ronald Bruce Turnbull. Brazil: BOVESPA, 1985.
Dawson, S. M. "The Trend Toward Efficiency for Less Development
    Stock Exchanges; Hong Kong." *Journal of Business Finance
    and Accounting* (Summer 1984): 151–161.
Dickie, Robert. "Development of Third World Securities Markets: An
    Analysis of General Principles and a Case Study of the Indone-
    sian Market." *Law & Policy in International Business* (1981):
    177–222.
Dipchang, Cecil R., Colin Dodds, Patricia McGraw, and Keng Chen.
    "Emerging Trends in China's Financial Sector." *Asian Pacific
    Journal of Management* Vol. 8, No. 1 (1991): 35–54.
Dong, Weiyuan. "Creating a Favorable Investment Environment."
    China Reconstructs (June 1987): 10–14.
Drake, P. J. "Securities Markets in Less Developed Countries." *Journal
    of Developmental Studies* (January, 1977): 72–91.
————. "Some Reflections and Problems Affecting Securities Mar-
    kets in Less Developed Countries." *Savings and Development*,
    1985: 5–15.
Duckworth, Michael. "Foreigners Divided Over Chinese Stocks." *Asian
    Wall Street Journal*. January 17, 1992.

Emerging Markets Data Base: Factbook. Capital Markets Department of International Finance Corporation, 1990.

Engle, Tom. "Stocks: New Domestic Financial Tool." *The China Business Review* (January–February 1986): 35–28.

Errunza, Vihang. "Efficiency and the Programs to Develop Capital Markets: The Brazilian Experience." McGill Working Paper 78–02, McGill University, 1978.

———. "Emerging Markets: A New Opportunity for Improving Global Portfolio Performance." *Financial Analysts Journal* (September–October 1983): 51–58.

Fei, John C. H., Ranis Gustav, and Shirley W. Y. Kuo. *Growth with Equity: The Taiwan Case.* New York: Oxford University Press, 1979.

Financial Times, various issues.

Fischer, William A. "Update on Enterprise Reforms." *The China Business Review* (September–October 1986): 42–45.

Gill, David. "Global Investing—The Emerging Markets." Paper presented at Council of Institutional Investors: Semi-annual Meeting in November 1987. Capital Markets Department of International Finance Corporation.

———. "The Influence of Emerging Capital Markets on Savings Mobilization in Latin American Countries." Prepared for Quarterly Review of the International Savings Banks Institute, the Capital Markets Department of International Finance Corporation, 1979.

Goldsmith, Raymond W. *Financial Structure and Development.* New Haven: Yale University Press, 1969.

———. "Capital Markets and Economic Development." Paper presented to the International Symposium on the Development of Capital Markets, Rio de Janeiro, September 1971.

Gray, Phillip. "India: A Review of Political, Economic and Stock Market Development." *Benefits & Compensation International* (September 1985): 2–17.

Grub, Phillip Donald, and Jian Hai Lin. *Foreign Direct Investment in China.* Westport, CT: Quorum Books, 1991.

Guide to China's Foreign Economic Relations and Trade, Policy Research Department and Foreign Economic Relations and Trade. Hong Kong: Economic Information Agency, 1983.

Gupta, L. C. *Rates of Return on Equities: The Indian Experience*. New Delhi, India: Oxford University Press, 1981.

Horch, Hans. "Finance Incentives for Securities Market Development: Brazil and Venezuela: Two Examples from the Latin American Experience." Paper presented at the OECD Capital Market Board Conference. Altinyunus, Turkey, July 1985.

Huan, Xiang. "China's Reforms Have Brought Rapid Growth." *EUROMONEY* (June 1985): 34–36.

Ignatius, Adi. "For Chinese Speculators, the Streets Offer Better Deals Than the Stock Exchange." *Wall Street Journal*, July 6, 1990: 4.

International Monetary Fund. *China: Economic Reform and Macroeconomic Management*. Washington, D.C.: International Monetary Fund, Occasional Paper No. 76, January 1991.

―――――. *Determinants and Systemic Consequences of International Capital Flows*. Occasional Paper. Washington, D.C.: International Monetary Fund, March 1991.

"In the Dragon's Eye." *Far Eastern Economic Review*, November 22, 1990: 49.

Jao, Y. C. "Financial Deepening and Economic Growth: A Cross Section Analysis." *The Malayan Economic Review* (June 1976): 47–57.

Jung, Woo S. "Financial Development and Economic Growth: International Evidence." *Economic Development and Cultural Change* (January 1986): 333–346.

Keynes, John Maynard. *The General Theory of Employment, Interest and Money*. New York: Harcourt Brace, 1936.

Khor, Hoe Ge. "China—Macroeconomic Cycles in the 1980s." *IMF Working Paper*. WP/91/85 (1991): 21.

Kim, Daniel C. "The Securities Exchange in a Developing Country: Evolution, Organization, Empirical Tests and Evaluation of Korea Stock Exchange." DBA dissertation, Kent State University, 1982.

Laurence, Martin M. "Some Efficiency Characteristics of the Kuala Lumpur and Singapore Stock Markets." Paper presented to the Financial Management Association Annual Meeting. Cincinnati, Ohio, October 1981.

Li, Qingyuan. "China's Infant Stock Markets." *Intertrade* (December 1990): 4–5.

Li, Shuzhong, and Guanghuai He. "A Look into Shenzhen's Stock Craze." *Intertrade* (April 1991): 26–27.

Lin, Zhiping, and Yow Ding. "An Assessment of China's Foreign Currency Exchange Markets." *Intertrade* (August 1991): 90–91.

Long, Millard. "A Note of Financial Theory and Economic Development." *Contribution of Finance to Development*. Washington, D.C.: World Bank Publications, 1985.

McGowan, Carl, and Woon Tam Wah. "Background Information for Stock Exchanges in Australia, Hong Kong, Japan and Singapore." Paper presented at the Academy of International Business Annual Meeting. New York, October 1985.

McKinnon, Ronald I. *Money and Capital in Economic Development.* Washington, D.C.: Brookings Institution, 1973.

————. "Financial Repression and the Liberalization Problem Within Less Developed Countries." In S. Grassman and E. Lundberg, eds., *The World Economic Order: Past and Prospects.* New York: St. Martin's Press, 1981.

Ness, Walter L., Jr. "Financial Market Innovation as a Development Strategy: Initial Results from the Brazilian Experience." *Economic Development and Cultural Change* (April 1975): 453–472.

"Old-style Banking Hinders Economy." *China Daily*, December 13, 1986.

Patrick, Hugh T. "Financial Development and Economic Growth in Underdeveloped Countries." *Economic Development and Cultural Change* (January 1966): 174–189.

Perkins, Dwight Heald. "Reforming China's Economic System." *Journal of Economic Literature* (June 1988): 601–640.

"Putting Banks on Road to Change." *China Daily*, November 3, 1986.

Rangarajan, C. "Financial Infrastructure and Economic Development." *Reserve Bank of India Bulletin* (February 1984): 71–79.

Samets, Arnold W. *Financial Development and Economic Growth: The Consequences of Underdeveloped Capital Markets.* New York: New York University Press, 1972.

Russo, Massimo. "Macroeconomic Adjustment and Reform in Planned Economies." *Working Paper*, WP/90/27, International Monetary Fund, 1990.

Samuels, J. M., and N. Yacout. "Stock Exchanges in Developing Countries." *Savings and Development* (1981): 217–230.

Schwartz, Robert, *Equity Markets: Structure, Trading, and Performance*. New York: Harper & Row, 1988.

Securities Markets in Asia and Oceania, 2nd edition. Asian Securities and Analysts Council, 1988.

"Shanghai Accepts Requests to Open Six Bank Branches." *Asian Wall Street Journal*, March 9, 1991: 10.

Shang, Ming. "Financial Reform in China: Process, Orientation and Sequence." Paper presented at the Asia Society in New York City, May 1987.

Shaw, Edward S. *Financial Deepening in Economic Development*. New York: Oxford University Press, 1973.

Shen, Jueren. "Structural Reforms Benefit Foreign Traders." *Intertrade* (January 1985): 11–12.

Shirreffe, David. "China's Latest Revolution." *EUROMONEY* (April 1985): 49–54.

Sudweeks, Brian L. "Equity Market Development in Developing Countries: General Principles, Case Studies, Portfolio Implications and Relevance for the People's Republic of China." Ph.D. dissertation, The George Washington University, 1987.

Sundararajan, V. "Financial Sector Reform and Central Banking in Centrally Planned Economies." *Working Paper*, WP/90/120, International Monetary Fund, 1990.

————. "Emerging Equity Market." Unpublished manuscript, 1988.

Tanzi, Vito. "Tax Reform in Economies in Transition: A Brief Introduction to the Main Issues." *Working Paper*, WP/91/23, International Monetary Fund, 1991.

Tseng, W., and M. Fetherston. *Recent Economic Development*, International Monetary Fund, October 1986.

van Agtmael, Antoine W. *Emerging Securities Market*. EUROMONEY Publications, 1984.

Virmani, Arvind. *Government Policy and the Development of Financial Markets: The Case of Korea*. Washington, D.C.: World Bank Staff Working Paper #747, 1985.

Volcker, Paul, Miguel Mancera, and Jean Godeaux. *Perspectives on the Role of a Central Bank*. International Monetary Fund, 1991.

Wai, U. Tun, and Hugh T. Patrick. "Stock and Bond Issues and Capital Markets in Less Developed Countries." *Capital Market in Less*

Developed Countries. International Monetary Fund (1973): 253–317.

Wei, Chun. "Enterprise Reform and the Role of Stock Markets." *Intertrade* (December 1990): 8–9.

Wilson, Dick. "China's Banks Learn a New Game." *The Banker* (August 1986): 14–27.

World Bank. *China: Economic Structure in International Perspective,* Annex 5 to *China: Long-term Development Issues and Options.* Washington, D.C.: World Bank Publications, 1985.

————. *China Finance and Investment.* Washington, D.C.: World Bank, March 1987.

————. *World Development Report.* New York: Oxford University Press, 1985–90.

————. *China: Country Economic Memorandum, Between Plan and Market.* Washington, D.C.: World Bank, May 8, 1990.

Wulf, Luc de. "Economic Reform in China." *Finance & Development* (December 1985): 19–22.

Xia, Bin. *China's Financial Markets in the Making.* Beijing, China: China Youth Publishing Company, 1987.

Yamanouchi, Kazuo. "The Chinese Price System and Thrust of Reform." *China Newsletter* No. 60 (1986): 2–11.

Yang, Peixin. "Molding a Socialist Financial Market." *Intertrade* (August 1985): Spectrum Supplement.

Yuan, Wen Qi. "Law of Value Cannot Be Denied." *Intertrade* (January 1985): 13–15.

Zhang, Guanghua. "Foreign Exchange Market Flourishes in Shanghai." *Intertrade* (March 1990): 28.

Zhao, Jinming. "Enterprises Raise Funds in a New Way." *China Daily,* July 25, 1986.

Index

Accounting and auditing, 100; principle, 121; standard, 147

Antoine W. van Agtmael, 12, 141, 145

Bank: commercial, 4; investment and trust, 47; loans, 29, 89; specialized, 29, 38, 39, 43, 49; state-owned, 83

Banker's acceptance, 52

Banking system, 28, 38, 42, 49

Board meeting, 99

Bond: construction, 41; corporate, 110; denominations, 83; enterprise, 60, 91; financial, 41, 60; government, 59, 61, 64; issuer, 75, 88, 91; maturity, 83, 85, 91; purchaser, 89; rates, 41; yields, 85, 91
—issuing, 81; cost, 84; regulation, 81

Bonds-in-kind incentive, 87

Brokerage firm, 120

Capital: accumulation, 133; cost, 82; long-term, 118; physical, 132

Central bank, 39, 49, 65, 104, 113; People's Bank of China, 38, 42

China International Trust and Investment Corporation (CITIC), 43

China's: capital market, 53; market capitalization, 100, 113, 118; reform effort, 127
—economic: external sector, 27; reform, 22, 101, 119; structure, 20, 21; system, 19
—financial: infrastructure, 37; reform, 35, 53; sector, 35, 37, 52, 120; system, 27, 36, 48, 53, 126
—secondary market activities, 103; participants, 74; securities market, 57, 101,

117, 122, 125; stock market, 93

Contractual savings institutions, 47; insurance company, 47; pension fund, 47

Credit rating service, 113, 122

Database systems, 128

Debt: debt-equity ratio, 143; external, 27; financing, 83

Demand-following approach, 140

Demand for financial services, 139

Developing countries, 4; experience, 146; high- and middle-income, 1; low-income, 1

Disclosure: financial information, 121; legislation, 122; requirement, 121

Disposable income, 125

Dividend: fixed amount of interest, 96; highest, 97; payment, 98; payment level, 99; variable, 97

Domestic: investment, 30; savings, 135, 136

Drake, P. J., 141

Economic development, 21, 145

Economic systems, 19; new, 22; prior to 1978, 19

Economy: barter, 135; centrally planned, 5, 20, 36; market, 137

Emerging securities market, 1; capitalization, 7; characteristics, 6; cumulative return, 8; financial system, 9; individ-

ual case study, 12; investor protection, 9; quality and visibility, 7

Enterprise: collectively owned, 71, 83; efficiency, 20; finaincial investment, 38; foreign investment, 73; joint-stock, 72; private, 20, 72; state-owned, 26, 69, 81, 92, 93, 119; stock-issuing, 95

Entrepreneurs, 141

Environment: favorable policy, 146; healthy economic, 144; stable political, 145

Equity: demand and supply, 145, 146; financing, 94; investment, 100; investors, 145; market, 142, 143, 144, 145

Equity market: benefit and cost, 144; contribution, 141; development, 144; Euro, 6; role, 141; viable, 147

External debt financing, 4

Face value, 104

Feile Acoustics Company, 108, 110

Financial assets, 134

Financial deepening, 134

Financial development, 39, 48, 57
—economic development, 134, 137; law, 139; path, 138; stage, 144

Financial instruments: certificate of deposit (CD), 48, 53; functions and characteristics,

48, 53; supply and demand, 146; treasury bond, 41

Financial institutions, 36; Agriculture Bank of China (ABC), 36, 39; Bank of China (BOC), 36, 39; Construction Bank of China (CBC), 36, 42; functions, 29, 36, 44; Industrial and Commercial Bank of China (ICBC), 42; Investment Bank of China (IBC), 43; nonbank, 46, 47; People's Bank of China (PBC), 36

Financial intermediaries, 135

Financial intermediation, 136, 140

Financial liberalization, 135

Financial market, 126

Financial repression, 134

Financial structuralist, 134

Financial systems: efficient, 28; functions, 53, 135; manipulation, 137; role, 141

Fixed asset, 94

Foreign: aid, 2; direct investment, in China, 27; investment in securities, 123, 125; trade, 27

Goldsmith, Raymond W., 137

Government: budget-financed investment, 57; intervention, 118, 142; policy regarding securities market, 1, 65, 122, 146

Growth of financial intermediation, 48

Guangdong, 61

Harrod-Domar model, 132

Indicator of financial deepening, 144

Institutional investor, 120, 126

Interbank: borrowing, 49, 50; market, 51; operations, 48

Interest-bearing loans, 29

Interest rate: bond, 83, 84; controls, 35; level and structure, 86

International debt crisis, 4

International Development Association (IDA), 3

International Finance Corporation (IFC), 3; capital market department, 12; emerging market database, 12

Investments: decision, 20; direction, 20; efficient allocation, 136; fiscal appropriation, 28; foreign, 12, 127; portfolio, 12, 127, 128; requirements of China's modernization program, 127; vehicles, 127

Joint stock enterprise, 72

Joint venture, 126

Level of economic development, 145

Listing: number, 105, 113; requirement, 105

Long, Millard, 135

McKinnon, Ronald I.: model, 133; analysis, 133

Maturity: bond, 85; borrowed fund, 50

Modernization program, 127
Monetary policy, 35, 36, 38, 42
Money market, 48, 52
Mutual funds, 128

Non-bank financial institutions,
  46, 47; emergence and
  growth, 46; investment and
  trust company, 46; leasing
  company, 46, 47

Open-door policy, 27
Ownership issue, 81, 93, 119

Patrick, Hugh T., 139, 145
Planning and price reform, 24
Pre-reform, 33, 38
Price: control, 104, 109; distor-
  tion, 85; movement, 112, 115
Pricing: mechanism, 107, 108;
  stock, 108
Primary market: development,
  81, 93

Reform: agriculture, 22; economic, 22, 36; financial, 28,
  35, 54; industrial, 24; planning and price, 24
Regional development banks:
  African Development Bank,
  3; Asian Development Bank,
  3; Inter-American Development Bank, 3
Regulatory agency, 66, 121
Regulatory framework, 121
Resource: efficient use, 21

Scarcity of fund, 82, 142
Secondary market, 84, 103, 104

Securities: attractiveness, 146;
  broker, 105, 120; clearing
  and delivery service, 103;
  company, 100; holders, 110;
  issuers, 74, 78; listed, 105;
  regulation, 62-67; standardized and quality, 7
Securities exchange: Shanghai
  (SSE), 113; Shenzhen, 115
Securities market: Chinese,
  117; contribution, 143; development, 118; emergence,
  119; importance, 101, 117;
  participants, 79; regulating
  and administrative agency,
  103; scope, 58
Settlement, 114; department,
  114; period, 114
Shanghai, 61, 113; Jing An
  Trading Center, 108, 109; Securities Exchange, 112, 123;
  trading centers, 103, 106
Shaw, Edward S., 132, 134
Shenyang Trading Center, 103,
  105, 109
Shenzhen: Development Bank,
  115; Securities Exchange,
  115, 123
Soviet Union, 20
State Council, 64
State-owned enterprise: financing, 74; large, 71; medium-
  and small-sized, 71; transforming, 93
Stock: demand, 146; dividend
  payment, 96, 98, 100; exchange, 103; issuer, 100; listing, 113; market, 144;
  purchaser, 110; real returns,

99; returns, 98
—issuing, 93; activities, 93,
99; amount, 95, 99; proce-
dure, 106, 111; purpose, 95,
96
Supply-leading finance, 139
Survey, 15

Tax policy, 122, 145, 146

Trading: activities, 103; centers,
103, 104, 105, 111; floor,
115; practice, 111; proce-
dure, 106, 111; regulation,
104; volume 110, 111

Wai, U. T., 141, 145

Yanzhong Industrial Company,
108, 110

About the Authors

MEI XIA is currently employed by the General Electric Information Services as a Senior Consulting Specialist. She also served as a Professorial Lecturer of International Business at the George Washington University and Market Analyst with the China National Cereals and Foodstuffs Import/Export Corporation.

JIAN HAI LIN is an Economist at the International Monetary Fund. Formerly, he was an Assistant Professor of International Finance at the George Washington University and Director of International Investment Banking at McMahan & Company. He is the author of numerous articles on international financial and trade matters and co-author of *Foreign Direct Investment in China* (Quorum Books, 1991).

PHILLIP D. GRUB is Professor of International Business and the holder of the Aryamehr Chair in Multinational Management at the George Washington University. During the past twelve years, he has spent a significant amount of time in China working with senior governmental officials at the national, provincial and state levels as well as with Chinese academicians on matters of economic development, academic programs, and foreign trade policy. In addition to 13 other books, he is the co-author of *Foreign Direct Investment in China* (Quorum, 1991).